Stains
le Temps perdu
Mln de Stains
Dugny
le Blanc-Mesnil
Double Courne du Nord
Fort de la Briche
la Briche
Maison de Seine
Villeneuve la Garenne
Palais de l'Elysée
Temple Anglican
Ambassade d'Angleterre
Champs Elysées
Av. Montaigne
Grand Palais des Beaux Arts
Petit
Musée de Galliera
Trocadero
Place d'Jena
Place de l'Alma
Quai de la Conférence
Concorde
S E I N E
Quai d'Orsay
Manufact. des Tabacs
Gare des Invalides
Magasin des Hôpitaux Mil.
Ecuries
St Pierre
Rue St Dominique
Hospice Leprince
Rue de Grenelle
Tour Eiffel
Champ de Mars
Ecole Militaire
Place Vauban
Tombeau de Napoléon 1er
Missions Etrangères
Rue de Babylone
St François-Xavier
Soeurs St Vinc. de Paul
Hôpital Laënnec
Pl. Dupleix
Pl. Fontenoy
Caserne
Place Cambronne
Pl. Breteuil
Ambassade de Russie
Ambass. d'Autriche-Hongrie
Bondy
Fort de Rosny
Fort de Nogent
Nogent sur-Marne
Bois de Vincennes
Champ de Manœuvre
Polygone
Charenton le Pont
St Maurice
Joinville le Pont
St Maur les-Fossés
Gentilly
Kremlin Bicêtre
Ivry sur-Seine
Alfort
Alfortville
Ft de Charenton
Charentonneau
Petit Créteil
Maisons-Alfort
Arcueil
Ft de Bicêtre
Ft d'Ivry
Port de Créteil
Pl. d'Italie
la Maison blanche
Parc de Montsouris
Conflans les Carrières
Bercy

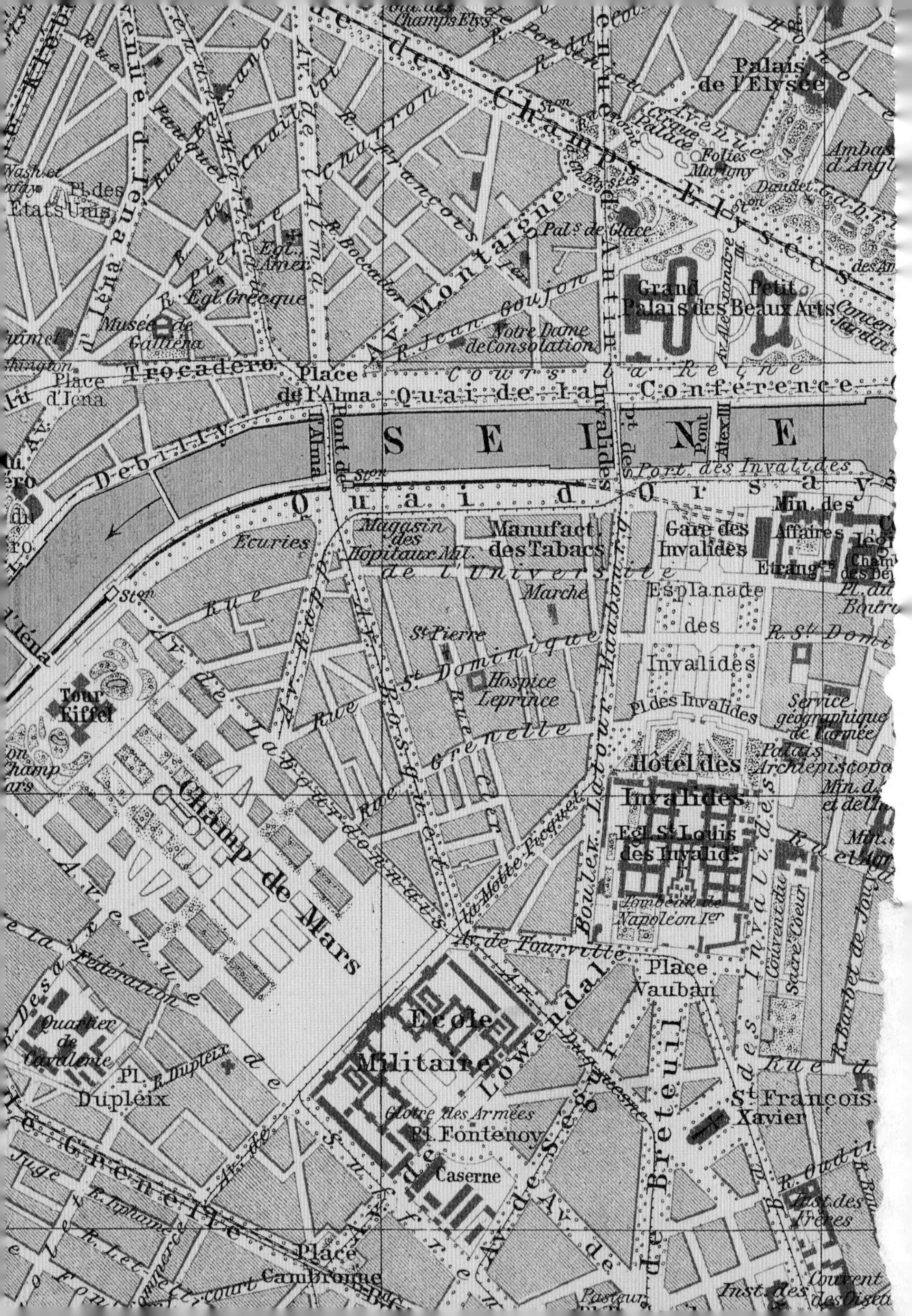

Palais de l'Elysée
Champs Elysées
Avenue des Champs Elysées
Cirque
Palace
Folies Marigny
Ambas. d'Angl.
Daudet
Av. Gabriel
Pl. des États Unis
Wash. et Lafay.
Avenue d'Iéna
Rue Bassano
R. Pierre Charron
R. François Ier
Egl. Amer.
R. Boccador
Av. de l'Alma
Egl. Grecque
Musée de Galliéra
Av. Montaigne
R. Jean Goujon
Notre Dame de Consolation
Pal.s de Glace
Grand Palais des Beaux Arts
Petit
Av. Alexandre III
Cours la Reine
Trocadéro
Place d'Iéna
Place de l'Alma
Quai de la Conférence
Quai Debilly
Pont de l'Alma
Seine
Pt. des Invalides
Pont Alex. III
Port des Invalides
Quai d'Orsay
Min. des Affaires Étrangères
Gare des Invalides
Manufact. des Tabacs
Magasin des Hôpitaux Mil.
Ecuries
de l'Université
Marché
Esplanade des Invalides
Rue
R. St. Dominique
St. Pierre
Rue St. Dominique
Hospice Leprince
Rue de Grenelle
Pl. des Invalides
Service géographique de l'armée
Palais Archiépiscopal
Tour Eiffel
Av. Rapp
Av. Bosquet
Rue Cler
Bd. Latour Maubourg
Av. de La Bourdonnais
Champ de Mars
Hôtel des Invalides
Egl. St. Louis des Invalid.s
Tombeau de Napoléon Ier
Av. de la Motte Picquet
Boulev.
Av. de Tourville
Place Vauban
Bd. des Invalides
Couvent du Sacré Coeur
R. Barbet de Jouy
Avenue de la Fédération
Quartier de Cavalerie
Pl. Dupleix
R. Dupleix
École Militaire
Av. Lowendal
Av. Duquesne
Gloire des Armées
Pl. Fontenoy
Caserne
Av. de Suffren
Av. de Breteuil
Av. de Ségur
St. François Xavier
Rue de Babylone
R. Oudinot
Inst. des Frères
Rue de Grenelle
R. Juge
R. Letellier
R. Tiphaine
Place Cambronne
Av. de Saxe
Couvent des Oiseaux
Inst.
Pasteur

# PARIS COCKTAILS

2ND EDITION

AN ELEGANT COLLECTION
OF OVER 100 RECIPES
INSPIRED BY THE CITY OF LIGHT

DONI BELAU

CIDER MILL PRESS
BOOK PUBLISHERS

*Paris Cocktails, 2nd Edition*

Copyright © 2023 by Cider Mill Press Book Publishers LLC.

This is an officially licensed book by Cider Mill Press Book Publishers LLC.

All rights reserved under the Pan-American and International Copyright Conventions.

No part of this book may be reproduced in whole or in part, scanned, photocopied, recorded, distributed in any printed or electronic form, or reproduced in any manner whatsoever, or by any information storage and retrieval system now known or hereafter invented, without express written permission of the publisher, except in the case of brief quotations embodied in critical articles and reviews.

The scanning, uploading, and distribution of this book via the internet or via any other means without permission of the publisher is illegal and punishable by law. Please support authors' rights, and do not participate in or encourage piracy of copyrighted materials.

13-Digit ISBN: 978-1-64643-301-8
10-Digit ISBN: 1-64643-301-7

This book may be ordered by mail from the publisher. Please include $5.99 for postage and handling. Please support your local bookseller first!

Books published by Cider Mill Press Book Publishers are available at special discounts for bulk purchases in the United States by corporations, institutions, and other organizations. For more information, please contact the publisher.

Cider Mill Press Book Publishers
"Where good books are ready for press"

501 Nelson Place
Nashville, Tennessee 37214

cidermillpress.com

"Joy Division" and "Sade's Taboo" from *Death & Co: Modern Classic Cocktails, with More than 500 Recipes* by David Kaplan, Nick Fauchald, and Alex Day, text copyright © 2014 by David Kaplan. Used by permission of Ten Speed Press, an imprint of the Crown Publishing Group, a division of Penguin Random House LLC. All rights reserved. Any third party use of this material, outside of this publication, is prohibited. Interested parties must apply directly to Penguin Random House LLC for permission.

Pages 1, 3-5, 14, 16-17, 21-22, 26, 29, 32, 39, 41-42, 46, 57, 60-61, 63, 65, 67-68, 74-75, 82, 84, 89, 95, 99, 107-109, 111, 117, 139, 141-143, 149, 151, 156, 160-161, 163, 167, 171, 174-175, 179, 183, 216, 237, 246-247, 253, 257-258, 260, 270-271, 273, 276, 286-287 used under official license from Shutterstock.com.

Pages 25, 48-49, 54-55, 58, 72, 90-91, 112, 118, 125, 127, 130, 135, 148, 158-159, 184, 187, 188 (top left), 195, 213-214, 218, 220, 225, 244, 264, 266, 278-279 by Doni Belau.

Pages 96-97 and 251 used under iStock image license.

All other photographs used courtesy of the respective establishments.

Printed in India

23 24 25 26 27 REP 5 4 3 2 1
First Edition

# - Contents -


Introduction + 5

J'Adore Paris Cocktails + 17

En Plein Air + 61

Du Vin + 75

Jazz Era Inspirations + 97

Casual and Creative Cocktails + 143

Joyeuse Holidays + 161

Artisanal Cocktails + 175

Francophile in the USA + 247

# INTRODUCTION

## There was then and there is now.

I've been coming to Paris since 1987 on an annual basis for weeks and now for months at a time. Back in those days, trying to get a barman to pour you a vodka on the rocks was so difficult; I once had to go back to the bar to point out the vodka bottle to the confused gent after three tries and three pours of gin on ice.

Then lightning hit, the cocktail heavens opened up and Romée de Gorianinoff and partners opened the Experimental Cocktail Club's speakeasy-style bar in 2007. La Conserverie and other craft bars opened in the following years, and now, craft cocktail culture is in full swing in Paris. You'll find that products are very carefully sourced; bitters, cordials and syrups are often handmade, and rums, whiskeys, and gins are macerated with exotic spices. This is the new "golden era" of Parisian cocktails—Parisians and visitors alike are waking up to a full-fledged cocktail craze.

Yet, is this entirely new? As the saying goes, what is old is new again. When Prohibition began in the States in 1919, some of the country's great bartenders hopped ship to Europe and became the Jazz Era's new mixologists. Frank Meier of the Ritz and Harry Craddock of the Savoy London come to mind. This was when the Bloody Mary, the French 75, and the Sidecar were invented, and you'll find a time much like now, when creativity was revered.

Think Hemingway packing a pistol and a strong drink or Cole Porter downing a bourbon after a night of playing.

Little known even by Parisian bartenders and bar owners is the fact that France actually has had a cocktail culture dating back to the 1800s. After talking to Stephen Martin at À La Française, who has been studying this issue for years now, I learned that in actuality France has had many hundreds of years relating in their own distinct way to their distilled liquors and liqueurs.

For the French palate three things are of utmost importance: alcohol is meant to go with food, balance in a drink is critical, and strong alcohol content in a drink feels alien and improper to them, because strong alcohol in France was typically used for medicinal purposes.

Take Chartreuse for example. Monks in the 1700s created Chartreuse Vert as a long life elixir. Bitters and eau de vies were taken for one's health or digestion often after a meal. In fact, there is a significant, age-old cultural difference in how the French perceive and understand liquor as opposed to how the Americans or the Brits comprehend it.

In France, liquor is not drunk to get drunk. So in essence, the idea of cocktailing is somewhat alien to them. The fact that the French don't like strong, alcohol-forward drinks doesn't make them newbie drinkers, rather it just shows that they come at the subject from a different perspective than an Anglo-Saxon. And I say, *vive la différence.*

At the turn of the century, cocktail bars were influenced greatly by expats and headquartered in the great hotels. Now the twenty- and thirty-somethings of France have embraced history only to remake it, in a more refined, more thoughtful way—and most importantly they are making this new cocktail culture much more accessible to the masses. We no longer just *prendre un verre* (have a glass), which in the past almost always meant wine. A French native today is open and anxious to try a French-made cocktail, chock full of French-made products.

With the exception of the five-star palace hotels, most of the well-made cocktails you'll sip in Paris are selling for 10 to 15 euros. That's expensive, it's true but it's still in the realm of reason when you consider the cost of the artisanal products that make up these creative cocktails and the time and care with which they are presented. We also hunted down a good batch of bars offering decent to excellent cocktails under 10 euros. And, to be sure, incredible things are still happening at the palace hotels. The Ritz and some of the newer five-star hotels have held their own due to wildly talented, professionally trained, passionate bartenders.

Today what we drink is art in a glass, and sipping these beauties turns a fun night of drinking into something exceptional and memorable. Fear not, for in our guide of Paris bars (new and historic) and Francophile bars in cities throughout the globe we have also included over 100 recipes so you can sample the artistry in your own home and bring a little corner of Paris into your life. For, where would we be without Paris?

### A Note About Ingredients (and Substitutions!)

The recipes in this book were taken verbatim from their creators. When a certain gin or rum is indicated, that brand was chosen by the mixologist because of the principles and the flavor profile of that liquor. The new craft bartenders take their ingredients very seriously, so if you want to replicate a drink exactly to be sure it tastes the same in your home as it does at the bar in Paris, use all the specific ingredients and brands listed. However, like a good mixologist will do when he or she runs out of something, feel free to substitute when necessary such as Absolut for Grey Goose vodka. Substituting your base liquor (e.g., gin, vodka, rum) with another premium brand is not going to hurt the outcome too much. However, having tasted the variety of different vermouths, liqueurs, and bitters (which is typically your secondary alcohol or flavor implement), there is a huge difference between them, and using a different brand in this case will make the drink taste quite different. Simply use your best judgment when substituting, and be sure to stock up on some key ingredients before tackling some of the more intricate recipes, like bitters and cordials! Happy mixing!

"If your arteries are good, eat more ice cream. If they are bad, drink more red wine. Proceed thusly."

*Sandra Byrd, Bon Appétit*

**SIMPLE SYRUP:** A number of cocktails call for simple syrup. Fortunately, simple syrup is as simple to make as its name suggests. Combine water and white granulated sugar in a 1:1 ratio in a pan over medium heat, stirring until sugar is completely dissolved. Do not boil. The syrup should keep for about a month in the fridge. You can add a dash of vodka to extend the shelf life.

## FRENCH COCKTAILING RULES

French love rules more than most cultures and as in everything else in French life, there are strict drinking guidelines to be followed.

**DO** clink glasses with everyone in the group, wishing each other "Santé"(to health).

**DO NOT** cross arms with others in your group—this brings bad luck.

**DO** make eye contact with the person whose glass you're clinking, or risk seven years of bad sex. Horrors!

**DO** bring a good bottle of Champagne to your hostess.

**DO NOT** open the Champagne before your guest of honor enters.

**ALWAYS** remember: moderation is a girl's best friend.

And the worst one, for me… Wait until your host pours you more wine.

P.S. I've always said rules were made to be broken.

**Apéritif/Dijestif:** A drink that stimulates your appetite or a drink that helps you digest your meal. Examples of apéritifs are Suze and soda, any Champagne-based cocktail, Lillet or a kir. Dijestifs are drinks made with brandy, Chartreuse, Bénédictine, or calvados.

**Bitters:** There are two different categories of bitters. There are bitter liqueurs, which are used as a modifier or base for a variety of cocktails. Examples include Campari, Suze, Aperol, Amaro, and Cocchi Rosa. There are also bitters, simply called *bitters,* which come in small bottles the most well known being Angostura bitters. These are infused and very flavorful alcohol-based liquids typically used in extremely small quantities to flavor a cocktail. They are made by a variety of companies and come in a myriad of flavors such as orange, chocolate, celery, and lavender, to name but a few.

> A NOTE ON BITTERS: Bitters are a key ingredient in today's craft cocktails. Stock up on a variety of flavors. There are a number of excellent companies making bitters in the U.S. and beyond including Bitter End, Fee's, Scrappy's, Bob's and Bittermans. Aromatic and orange are the most common flavor profiles. A sampler pack, which several of the companies offer, is a great idea.

**Cordials:** A sweetened and flavored liquor. Cordials and liqueurs are basically the same thing, except in the UK where a cordial is a sweet syrup without alcohol.

**Liqueur:** An alcoholic substance that is typically sweeter than a liquor and made by combining a distilled spirit with something sweet and flavorful such as fruit, coffee, cream, chocolate, herbs, or spices. Examples are Cassis, Kahlúa, Irish cream, crème de menthe, and Grand Marnier.

**VERMOUTH:** Vermouth is an aromatized, fortified wine that can be white, amber, rose, or red. Historically, vermouth coming from Italy was sweet and from France was dry, but now manufactures all over make a range of colors and versions in response to consumer appetite.

**LIQUOR:** Alcoholic substance made from grains, plants, or sugar cane and fermented to be drunk straight or combined and used as the base of a cocktail. Examples are rum, vodka, gin, brandy, tequila, whiskey, and cachaça (a sugar cane–based alcohol made in Brazil).

**GRENADINE:** A popular pomegranate juice and sugar syrup used in cocktails. It can easily be made at home, which results in a better end-product than bottled versions. However, if you don't have the time for DIY, almost all syrups all available over the counter.

## WHAT IS THE CRAFT BAR MOVEMENT ALL ABOUT, REALLY?

Take the locavore movement, the artisanal quest, the DIY urge, and an ever-increasingly sophisticated palate. Combine that in a cocktail shaker with hundreds of specialized small-batch products made in France, garnish with passion and artistry, and you've got the Parisian craft bar movement.

It didn't start here, but with hundreds of years of experience distilling specialty liquors and liqueurs, France was ripe and waiting to fall head over heels into the movement. As Romée and his co-founders Olivier Bon and Pierre-Charles Cros from the Experimental Cocktail

Club group believed, if France has the best wine and food in the world, why not cocktails?

But Rome wasn't built in a day, and I don't want to give short shrift to those whose shoulders these new bartenders (both men and women) stand on. The guys from Le Grand Hotel bar, the Ritz, and of course Harry's New York bar were the beginners, then Le Forum opened in the '30s and Rosebud followed in the '60s.

Then in the 1990s, Buddha Bar hit the Parisian stage and almost singlehandedly was responsible for reintroducing exotic drinks and, more importantly, creating a global chic environment. Remember those lounge CDs that were an essential part of your CD collection, back when you actually had CDs?

The true beginning of the craft cocktail movement can be traced to 2000 when Milk and Honey opened in New York City and later to

2005 when Audrey Saunders opened the Pegu Club in Manhattan. All of these mixologists set the stage for 2007 when Experimental Cocktail Club opened in Paris just one year after Death & Company began in New York City in 2006. Paris and New York City drinkers were blown away by these adventurous bars that brought back the vintage look and feel of speakeasy days while putting a creative twist on the old recipes and revealing something entirely new.

Now bartenders are becoming as focused, diligent, and inventive as the most creative chefs in Paris, New York, London, Los Angeles, and beyond. They are using alcohol made from yogurt or tobacco, or infusing traditional alcohols with unusual spices or herbs. They are making their own shrubs, syrups, cordials, and bitters. Some of the most impressive drinks I tried were made with little-known fresh herbs, small-batch liqueurs and liquors; dehydrated orange or lemon slices or powdered dehydrated tomato laced around the rim of a Bloody Mary.

The garnishes have become terribly creative, pinned on with mini clothespins, referencing literature, or in a slight overstatement, set on fire. The creative cocktail wave encouraged the best of the city's bartenders to begin mixing unusual ingredients with home-made products to create something sublime.

Everyone I met while researching this book had a passion for cocktail invention. While only a select few achieved a drink of Picasso or Matisse status, all are continuing to create with zeal. Gone are the days when a bar stool was simply a place to sit down and tell a guy your troubles while he poured you something strong. Now it's very tasty theatre, where bartender and patron alike are learning something new every day.

# J'ADORE PARIS COCKTAILS

AMOUR À LA FRANÇAISE 20
SUZE AND SODA 24
LE METRO 27
CHAMPAGNE STILETTO 28
FRENCH 75 30
TREIZE 75
COOKIE LOVE SHOTS 34
ALCHIMIA COCKTAIL 37
VERBENA COCKTAIL 40
PARK HYATT PURPLE MOJITO 43
PARIS PARIS 44
B&B 47
OH MY DOG 50
100% WINTER VITAMIN 51
LA SAUVAGE BEE'S KNEES 56
RAPHAEL 59

Going to over fifty bars in six weeks might not be everyone's idea of a good time, but I dare say a better education cannot be had if you really want to learn about the nature of bartending as it stands now in Paris. It's being called the "New Golden Age of Cocktails," and one cannot disagree considering how much passion, effort, sourcing and sheer love are being put into mixing these libations. These particular recipes are an homage to the most beautiful city on Earth. Cheers to drinking Paris in a glass!

"THE BEST OF AMERICA DRIFTS TO PARIS. THE AMERICAN IN PARIS IS THE BEST AMERICAN. IT IS MORE FUN FOR AN INTELLIGENT PERSON TO LIVE IN AN INTELLIGENT COUNTRY. FRANCE HAS THE ONLY TWO THINGS TOWARD WHICH WE DRIFT AS WE GROW OLDER—INTELLIGENCE AND GOOD MANNERS."

*F. Scott Fitzgerald*

# — AMOUR À LA FRANÇAISE —

It's only appropriate to begin this section with a cocktail conceived at Bar le Forvm, a historically important institution opened in 1931 and run by the same family until recently closing its doors for good.

---

- **1⅓ oz. brandy**
- **¾ oz. ginger liqueur**
- **1 tablespoon fresh lemon juice**
- **1 tablespoon simple syrup**
- **4 dashes crème de Cassis**
- **1 egg white**

---

**METHOD:** Shake all ingredients, without ice, in cocktail shaker to incorporate egg white with ingredients. Add ice and shake again before straining into chilled glass.

**SERVING SUGGESTION:** Serve in a Nick and Nora glass (a mini-martini glass with a rounded bottom) with a lemon twist.

"EVEN THE PIGEONS ARE
DANCING, KISSING,
GOING IN CIRCLES, MOUNTING
EACH OTHER.
PARIS IS THE CITY OF LOVE,
EVEN FOR THE BIRDS."

*Samantha Schutz,*
*I Don't Want To Be Crazy*

# French Films Party

If you're not able to be in Paris, what better way to pretend that you're there than watching some classic French films and letting the dialogue wash over you as you sip on some cinephile-inspired cocktails?

*Amélie:* The title character in this adorable and hugely popular film fixes her friend a Kir, dry white wine topped with Crème de Cassis. Why not do the same for your friend, and yourself? Kir St. Louis (page 78)

*The 400 Blows:* The story of young Antoine Doinel is not one of tipsy swagger, but it is a seminal work in French New Wave cinema, and you can honor Antoine's love of milk and his vanishing innocence with a sweet cocktail. Cookie Love Shots (page 34)

*Mon Oncle:* The garish trappings of modernity get a brilliant send-up in this film about an uncle who prefers a cycle through central Paris with his nephew over an automated fish fountain. Safe to assume he'd prefer the simplicity of a classic cocktail over a newfangled concoction topped with foam. French 75 (page 30)

# — SUZE AND SODA —

Suze, one of the better known French brands of gentian-based bitters, has been around since the late 1800s and won a prestigious gold medal at the 1889 World's Fair in Paris.

- 1 part Suze
- 3 parts soda water

**METHOD:** Pour Suze and then soda into a rocks glass with ice.

**SERVING SUGGESTION:** Garnish with an orange wedge.

> A rocks glass, or a low-ball glass, is the type of glass in which a vodka, scotch, or a whiskey on the rocks is served, hence the name.

*Bonheur, je te fais une grande place dans ma vie.*

HAPPINESS. I MAKE A BIG SPACE FOR YOU IN MY LIFE.

METROPOLITAIN

# — LE METRO —

My friend Dana, who feels terribly lucky to be working as an American in France, created this one in honor of the fastest way to get around town.

---

- **2 oz. high-quality French brandy or Cognac (a very high-quality brandy is imperative)**
- **1 oz. cassis**
- **½ oz. lemon juice**
- **Several dashes of Pechaud bitters**
- **Morello cherries (or your favorite premium cherries)**

---

**METHOD:** Shake all ingredients with ice in a cocktail shaker and strain into an ice-cold martini glass and garnish with two Morello cherries.

# — CHAMPAGNE STILETTO —

This cocktail was created by cocktail expert Forest Collins of 52Martinis at the request of Cara Black to celebrate the 20th anniversary of her Aimée Leduc 90's era detective series. Her fierce female lead solves murder mysteries in each Paris arrondissement and also has a penchant for leather stiletto boots and Champagne. (But we won't tell if you decide to sub in sparkling wine instead!)

- **1 oz. Rittenhouse 100 Rye (or your preferred overproof rye)**
- **2 teaspoons simple syrup**
- **Champagne to top**

**METHOD:** Pour rye and simple syrup into aChampagne flute that has been chilled in the freezer. Express a lemon peel over the glass so the oils spray inside. Top with Champagne.

**ALTERNATIVE:** Add 3 teaspoons freshly squeezed lemon juice for a brighter and more acidic version.

# — FRENCH 75 —

This cocktail dates back to 1915 and its original name "Soixante-Quinze" referred to the French 75 mm field gun heavily in use during WWI. Over the years, the name morphed to "75" and then "French 75" and the recipe has changed even more over the last century. While gin has historically been the common element in the many different versions of this drink, we like the modern day Cognac take.

---

- **1 oz. Cognac**
- **¼ oz. simple syrup**
- **Champagne**
- **½ oz. fresh lemon juice**

---

**METHOD:** Shake all ingredients except the Champagne with ice and strain into a flute. Top with Champagne.

# — TREIZE-75 —

Treize co-owner, Kajsa von Sydow, created this one after drinking too many bad versions of this classic cocktail.

- **1¾ oz. spiced honey infused gin**
- **¾ oz. freshly squeezed and strained lime juice**
- **¾ oz. simple syrup**
- **Champagne (preferably brut)**

**METHOD:** Add gin, lime juice and simple syrup to shaker half full with ice cubes. Shake and strain into a coupe. Top with Champagne. Garnish with a maraschino cherry.

"COCKTAILS ARE OFTEN NAMED AFTER PEOPLE OR EVENTS, AND THE 'SOIXANTE-QUINZE' WAS OFTEN A SYMBOL OF HOPE IN BATTLE, SOMETHING THAT WE STILL NEED TODAY. BRITISH NOVELIST ALEC WAUGH DUBBED IT 'THE MOST POWERFUL DRINK IN THE WORLD', WHILE HARRY CRADDOCK ADDED 'HITS WITH REMARKABLE PRECISION' TO HIS RECIPE IN THE SAVOY COCKTAIL BOOK. MOST BARS HAVE GONE OLD SCHOOL, SERVING IT AGAIN IN COLLINS GLASSES THAT RESEMBLES THE 75 MM CARTRIDGE SHELL--THE HEMINGWAY BAR EVEN KEEPS ONE OF THOSE ON A SHELF FOR COMPARISON. PERSONALLY I PREFER TO SERVE IT IN A FLAT CHAMPAGNE GLASS, AS IT WAS SIPPED BY HUMPHREY BOGART AND INGRID BERGMAN IN CASABLANCA; THAT OLD WORLD CLASSINESS AND STYLE SPEAKS TO MY HEART."

*Kajsa von Sydow*

# — RITZ SIDECAR —

Although the Sidecar was likely invented in London, it was popularized at the famous Harry's bar in Paris in the 20s. Today it's also one of the more famous cocktails made at the Ritz (see Bar Hemingway at the Ritz Paris, page 133). Recipe courtesy of Colin Peter Field, Ritz Hotel.

---

- **2½ oz. Cognac**
- **1½ oz. triple sec or Cointreau**
- **1 oz. fresh lemon juice**

---

**METHOD:** Stir all ingredients together in a mixing glass with ice and strain into a chilled martini glass. Garnish with a lemon twist.

"IF A LADY IS WEARING BLACK, I'LL GIVE HER A RED OR WHITE ROSE AS A GARNISH FOR HER DRINK. IF SHE'S EXOTIC, I'LL PUT AN ORCHID IN HER COCKTAIL."

+++

**COLIN PETER FIELD, HEAD BARTENDER AT THE RITZ AND AUTHOR OF *BAR HEMINGWAY***

# — COOKIE LOVE SHOTS —

When you combine the talents of local boaker Jean Hwang Carrant of Cookie Love and one of the Paris best bartenders, Joseph Akhavan, you get this delicious result. This recipe makes about 8 shots to share with friends!

---

- **3 oz. rhum**
- **4 oz. almond milk**
- **3 teaspoons maple syrup**
- **Mini cookies for garnish**

---

**METHOD:** combine and chill liquid ingredients and then pour into shot glasses that you top with a mini cookie.

# Hotel Bars

## Shangri-La

**10 Avenue d'Iéna, 75116 Paris**
**Phone: 01 53 67 19 93**
**Price: *****
**Atmosphere: Sophisticated**
**http://www.shangri-la.com/paris/**

Drinks here will set you back some, but remember you'll be drinking in the former palace of Prince Roland Bonaparte, the grand-nephew of Napoleon (yes, *that* Napoleon). Don't go to the bar itself; instead, walk in boldly as if you were a guest and sit in one of the many intertwining rooms to your right. These were the palace's former parlor rooms and you'll find many comfortable places to sit. This is a beautiful area to have tea, but if you are ready for your cocktail, a waiter will come running. Order their 1896, a Champagne cocktail that honors the year the palace was built. Dress appropriately, drink slowly, and enjoy thoroughly.

"I DRINK CHAMPAGNE WHEN I WIN,
TO CELEBRATE.
AND I DRINK CHAMPAGNE WHEN I
LOSE, TO CONSOLE MYSELF."
—*Napoleon Bonaparte*

## Georges V

**33 Avenue George V, 75008 Paris**
**Phone: 01 53 23 78 52**
**Price: *****
**Atmosphere: Regal**
**http://www.fourseasons.com/paris/dining/lounges/le_bar/**

I've always maintained that paying 25 euros or more for a cocktail here simply to sit among the incredible floral displays is worth it. Sometime back in 1999 Jeff Leatham, an American from Utah, was appointed head florist for the Four Seasons Georges V Hotel. The budget he was given was all but limitless. If you can imagine it, flowers appear here as theatre. They *will* take your breath away. And because it's the Four Seasons and one of the great hotels in Paris, the drinks will satisfy you, too. I prefer a Champagne cocktail when I'm here because I want to feel like a princess in these surroundings.

## Bar 228 at the Meurice

**228 Rue de Rivoli, 75001 Paris**
**Phone: 01 44 58 10 66**
**Price:** ***
**Atmosphere: Perfect for planning how to conquer the world**
**www.lemeurice.com/**

Decorated like an English gentleman's club, you can hole up here sipping your cocktail while pondering how you'll conquer the world. Or enjoy the Philippe Starck–designed lobby and have a drink in one of the comfy chairs.

"To err is human.
To loaf is Parisian."

*Victor Hugo*

## Peninsula Hotel

**19 Avenue Kléber, 75116 Paris**
**Phone: 1 58 12 28 88**
**Price:** ***
**Atmosphere: Grandiose**
**http://paris.peninsula.com**

You have an embarrassment of choices at the Peninsula Hotel in terms of where to raise your glass. There's the rooftop terrace, the bar Kléber and the cigar lounge for after-dinner whiskey drinks, dijestifs and important discussions. With five-star service and cocktails, with your platinum card in hand you can't go wrong.

## Le Royal Monceau

**37 Avenue Hoche, 75008 Paris**
**Phone: 01 44 58 10 66**
**Price:** ***
**Atmosphere: Smart Upscale**
**http://www.leroyalmonceau.com/**

Designed by Starck and owned by Raffles, this palace hotel, which was opened in 1928, boasts an expansive bar made up of several rooms and a terrace, surprisingly subtle for Starck. But what's hiding in plain sight are some superbly delicious cocktails. I was

# — ALCHIMIA COCKTAIL —

Alchimia is the Italian word for *alchemy,* and there is no doubt that this cocktail gets it right.

- **1¾ oz. Russian Standard Platinum Vodka**
- **½ oz. cassis (preferably Mickael Antolin brand)**
- **½ oz. galangal syrup (see instructions below)**
- **¾ oz. fresh lemon juice**
- **1¼ oz. infusion of lemon balm, verbena, cinnamon, and orange peel**

**METHOD:** Vigorously shake all of the ingredients in a cocktail shaker with ice to make a nice foam, then pour into a martini glass.

**TO MAKE GALANGAL SYRUP:** Add some slices of galangal to your simple syrup while boiling. When creating the syrup, let stand for as long as possible to soak up the taste.

**TO MAKE THE INFUSION:** Put the fresh herbs, spices, and orange peel in boiling water, remove the pan from heat, and let it steep like tea. The longer you steep the more fragrant the infusion. Cool before using.

**SERVING SUGGESTION:** Garnish with one cucumber slice and fresh verbena leaves.

wowed by my tasting at this bar, starting with the Singapore Sling (page 113), thankfully made less sweet than the norm.

Then I tasted the Verbena Cocktail (page 40), designed to celebrate spring and poured from a teapot. The herbal flavor mixing with the vodka and the citrus is a happy combination indeed.

## Bar Josephine at Lutetia Hotel

**45 Bd Raspail, 75006 Paris**
**+33 1 49 54 46 00**
**Price:** ****
**Ambience: Luxury hotel**

Who doesn't want to drink in the same space that has hosted Picasso, James Joyce and Josephine Baker? This historical institution has not only seen many famous patrons, but was requisitioned by the Nazi's in WWII. After a few years' closure, this left bank art nouveau hotel reopened to much fanfare, and a visit to their Bar Josephine is a great way to get in to check out the changes. The bar wows with expansive frescos and large windows that let in loads of light. Of course, it's spendy, but you're paying for the historical space, beautiful decor, delicious drinks and attentive service. Plus they have a "martini-o'clock" section on their menu! Early evening bar snack menu includes sushi, sashimi, maké and rolls and it's worth checking their calendar for free jazz nights.

## 1802

**22 Rue Pascal, 75005 Paris**
**+33 1 40 09 09 09**
**Price:** ***
**Atmosphere: Boutique hotel rum bar**
**bar1802.com/fr/**

Rum just keeps getting more popular globally and has always had a special place in the hearts of the French, considering that much of it is made in the Islands that belong to the overseas departments and territories. This lovely little boutique hotel bar, located in the chic 4 star Monte Cristo, highlighting this delicious. They offer a selection of rum, rhum and cocktails featuring both. If you will be spending extended time in Paris, they also have a private rum club.

# — VERBENA COCKTAIL —

Created at the Le Royal Monceau, Paris.

- **1¾ oz. Beefeater 24 gin infused with verbena leaves**
- **1 tablespoon lavender syrup**
- **2 teaspoons Velvet Falernum**
- **1 oz. apple juice**

**TO INFUSE THE GIN:** Infuse 1 liter of gin with ¼ cup of lemon verbena leaves for at least 24 hours but up to 4 days. Strain before using.

**TO MAKE LAVENDER SYRUP:** Make simple syrup but add a dried handful of lavender flowers while boiling the sugar, let steep, strain, and use once cold.

Now you'll be ready to make several Verbena Cocktails. To make one, put all the ingredients in a small pitcher and mix them with ice.

**SERVING SUGGESTION:** Let the recipient pour over ice in a rocks glass with fresh verbena leaves and large ice cubes.

## Park Hyatt Vendome

**19 Avenue Kléber, 75116 Paris**
**Phone: 1 58 71 10 60**
**Price: *****
**Atmosphere: Slick chic**
**http://paris.vendome.hyatt.com**

Somewhere between slick and cozy, catering to a crowd of hotel guests and Parisians, the bar at the Vendome Hotel will never remind you of a Hyatt back home. This is a five-star experience, and the cocktail prices, which run from 27 to 30 euros, will prove it. Sit at the bar to enjoy the extremely experienced barmen and women who will present you with truly unique drinks. I tried the Bramble & Queen (page 119) served in one of the most gorgeous coupe glasses I've ever seen. This drink incorporates ylang ylang water and will transport you to an exotic beach in Asia.

## — PARK HYATT PURPLE MOJITO —

For the past few decades, mojitos were the go-to cocktails for Parisians. And while in the early days of the revival many craft bars would avoid making this mainstream drink, Yann Daniel, former barman at the Park Hyatt, took a different approach and created something artisanally accessible.

---

- **4 fresh blackberries**
- **12 mint leaves**
- **Half of a fresh lime**
- **2 barspoons of brown sugar**
- **Soda water**
- **1 tablespoon violet syrup (or crème de violette)**
- **1¾ oz. Bacardi reserve dark rum**

---

**METHOD:** Muddle the blackberries, the mint leaves, lime, and sugar together with a little bit of soda water in a high-ball glass. Pour in the violet syrup and the dark rum. Fill the glass with crushed ice and top off with soda water.

**SERVING SUGGESTION:** Stir it with a barspoon, and add mint leaf garnish and two straws (two straws make it easier to continue the muddling action on your own).

# — PARIS PARIS —

This cocktail was created by the talented team at the Bar Josephine in the iconic Hotel Lutetia.

- **1 oz. Vodka Guillotine**
- **⅔ oz. St-Germain**
- **½ oz. soda**
- **2 ¾ oz. Taittinger Champagne**
- **1 oz. citrus shrubb**

**METHOD:** Build the drink in a Collins glass over ice and stir.

"THE JOSEPHINE BAR IDENTIFIES WITH ONE OF THE MOST LIBERAL, ORIGINAL, FANTASTIC AND EMANCIPATED ICONS OF THE ROARING TWENTIES IN FRANCE."

+++

**NICOLA BATTAFARANO,**
**HEAD BARMAN**

0
200m
500m
1 km
Plans-Guides Blay, 26 rue Feydeau
75002 PARIS
O
E
S
Quai du Maréchal Joffre
PT. DE LEVALLOIS
Quai
Rue
PT. DE LEVALLOIS
BÉCON
LA COURNEUVE
93 SEINE ST. DENIS
DRANCY
AUBERVILLIERS
BOBIGNY
19
Buttes Chaumont
NOISY-LE-SEC
ROMAINVILLE
MONTREUIL
R. Ernest Cognacq
Rue Marius
Antonin
Paul
Kléber
Aufan
Rue Danton
Villa Chaptal
Rue Chaptal
Rue Barbès
N 308
R. de Rouvray
Boulevard
Victor
Villiers
Rue Vergniaud
Bineau
Hugo
Parmentier
Perronet
Rue Delaizement
HAUTS DE SEINE
BOIS
PTE MAILLOT
Maillot
Avenue
Suresnes
Lac
INFÉRIEUR
VICTOR-HU
Victor
Raymond
St Cloud
Henri
Martin
LA MUETTE
R. DE LA POMPE

# — B&B —

This equal parts brandy and Bénédictine digestif has been around for nearly a century. Bénédictine created a bottled version of the combo (making it one of the first bottled cocktails ever!) and you can still buy it today. But, it's easy to make at home, which also allows for adjustment of proportions to your taste.

- **1 part Bénédictine liqueur**
- **1 part Brandy**

**METHOD:** mix equal parts Bénédictine and brandy and serve on the rocks, shaken on ice and straight up or in a snifter at room temp, as is your preference.

> Bénédictine liqueur made in France has been imported to the States since the late 1800s but was created in the early part of the 1500s by a Bénédictine monk as a medicinal tonic. Bénédictine was used in a popular vintage drink, the B&B, created in the 1930s.

## Le Quatre

**Buddha Bar Hotel, 4 Rue d'Anjou, 75008 Paris**
**Phone: 01 83 96 88 70**
**Price: *****
**Atmosphere: Exclusive & intimate**
**buddhabarhotelparis.com/**

The bar inside the Buddha Bar Hotel was designed to be very different than the über-famous original Buddha Bar, which is around the corner. The original that opened in 1996 with the gigantic Buddha is a huge place with setups behind the bar for up to five bartenders. Now there are fourteen Buddha bars worldwide. This iconic place is nearly single-handedly responsible for the Lounge CD trend that was omnipresent in the late 1990s and early 2000s. You can enjoy tea here in the afternoon and some killer drinks at night, such as their popular Oh My Dog. In fine weather, take your drink in the beautiful courtyard and say a toast of gratitude.

## — OH MY DOG —

This popular cocktail is served at both the Buddha Bar Paris and the Buddha Bar Hotel bar, Le Quatre.

---

- **1¾ oz. gin infused with white pepper**
- **½ oz. Grenade liquor**
- **½ tablespoon Belvoir raspberry and rose cordial**
- **Ginger ale to top**
- **Grenadine**
- **Wedge of fresh lime**

---

**METHOD:** To infuse gin with white pepper, place ½ tablespoon of white peppercorns (broken) in 1 liter bottle of gin for 5 hours. Strain before using.

Combine infused gin, grenadine, and cordial in a cocktail shaker with ice, shake, strain, and serve with ice in a lovely tumbler topping with ginger ale.

**SERVING SUGGESTION:** Garnish with a shake of grenadine and fresh lime.

> Belvoir produces a delightful raspberry and rose cordial made in the UK that you can get in the States. In this case, the word cordial is used to identify a sweet, non-alcoholic drink. If you cannot find it in your region, substitute a drop of rosewater and several crushed raspberries, being careful to strain out the seeds before serving over ice and topping off with the ginger ale.

# — 100% WINTER VITAMIN —

This actually feels healthy when you drink it, thanks to the guys at the Buddha Bar Paris. Serve at brunch.

- **1¾ oz. vodka**
- **2 teaspoons Cynar**
- **2 teaspoons Aperol**
- **2 teaspoons honey (or less if you don't like it very sweet)**
- **2 teaspoons fresh lime**
- **2 barspoon apricot/yuzu jam**
- **1¾ oz. juice made from fresh carrot and fresh apple (half and half—store-bought juice is fine)**
- **2 dashes of celery bitters**

**METHOD:** Shake all ingredients with ice, strain, and serve in a small carafe or soup style.

**SERVING SUGGESTION:** Top with finely chopped carrot shavings and green leaves such as coriander or parsley.

> Cynar, similar to Campari, is a bitter liqueur made in Italy from artichokes as well as other ingredients. Don't worry, it doesn't taste like artichokes!

# Superb Ambiance

## Treize au Jardin

**5 Rue de Médicis, 75006 Paris**
**Price** **
**Atmosphere: Floral down-home goodness**
**treizeaujardin.com**

Treize ticks a lot of boxes: tea parlor, brunch spot, restaurant, bakery and day drinking stop extraordinaire. It's a home away from home from the creative and talented duo of Kajsa von Sydow and Laurel Sanderson. These two put a lot of heart and soul into everything they do so expect tasty comfort food, decor and drinks! Here's where you go for creative and fun cocktails like the "tea" for two (G&T served in a pot with 2 teacups). They also make delicious non-alcoholic drinks too. A stop on their lovely terrace across from the Luxembourg gardens in a must for a sunny Paris day.

"I've got lots of good friends. I could have affairs. I can read a book all night, put the cat on the end of the bed. I can pick up my passport and go to France. I don't have to ask anybody."

—*Joanna Lumley*

## Ciel de Paris

**33 Avenue du Maine, 75015 Paris**
**56th floor**
**Phone: 0 1 40 64 77 64**
**Price:** ***
**Atmosphere: Elite view**
**cieldeparis.com/**

If you want Champagne and a city view, this is the best place in town. You'll also find an impressive array of Champagne by the glass from 13 to 30 euros as well as Bellini's, including one Champagne cocktail with mandarin and ginger.

## La Belle Hortense

**31 rue Vieille du Temple, 75004 Paris**
**Phone: 01 42 74 59 70**
**Price:** **
**Atmosphere: Literary chic**
**cafeine.com/belle-hortense**

This has been one of my favorite bars for forever. It's small and terribly French, with the fantasy bohemian French chic décor that we all love—plus it's a bookstore. To me, this is a naturally perfect combination. The owner, Xavier Denamur, has about six places around Paris including two more on the same street; each has its own flavor but every one is similarly charming. (See website for details.)

### Lapérouse

**51 Quai des Grands Augustins, 75006 Paris**
**Phone: 1 43 26 68 04**
**Price:** ***
**Atmosphere: Late-night rendez-vous**
**laperouse.com/**

This 250-plus-year-old bar and restaurant is famous not only for its extremely beautiful interior but also for its private rooms upstairs. This is where the gentlemen of the day used to bring their courtesans or mistresses and give them diamonds to keep them bejeweled. You'll see scratch marks still on the old mirrors in these elite little private rooms because the mademoiselles wanted to be sure the diamonds were indeed real.

### La Recyclerie

**83 Boulevard Ornano, 75018 Paris**
**Phone: 01 42 57 58 49**
**Price:** *
**Atmosphere: Eco-friendly**
**larecyclerie.com/**

Although not situated in the most pristine area of Paris, this restaurant/bar/farm is buzzing with life inside the old train station it calls home. During the summer, sip your cocktails on the long stretch of terrace that parallels the old railroad tracks and enjoy this eclectic and creative space in Montmartre.

### L'Apicius

**20 Rue d'Artois, 75008 Paris**
**Phone: 1 43 80 19 66**
**Price:** ***
**Atmosphere: Refined**
**restaurant-apicius.com/**

Situated in a corner of the 8th arrondissement in a beautiful mansion from the 1860s is a Michelin Star restaurant and a very chic bar with a tiny terrace that you can enjoy even if you aren't prepared to pay for a meal here. The 19th-century frescoed ceilings in

Maker's Mark
JIM BEAM
SOUTHERN COMFORT
Mardi
17
Février

BROOKLYN LAGER
HENDRICK'S

the bar somehow meld perfectly with the modern, dramatic décor, but the real star here, eclipsing the gorgeous surroundings, are the *sur mesure* cocktails prepared by the talented *chef du bar,* Valentin. Tell him or the bar manager Jil what you are in the mood for; don't be too specific but do try to challenge them. Or try their farm-to-glass Bloody Mary, made with cherry tomatoes smashed and strained in front of your eyes with BBQ bitters and cranberries. Yes, I said it: cranberries?! You'll never taste anything else like it. Refreshing, smoky, salty, and not nearly as thick as some Bloody's—this is a triumph!

## L'ÉCLAIR

**32 Rue Cler, 75007 Paris**
**Phone: 1 44 18 09 04**
**Price:** **
**Atmosphere: Cozy & bohemian**
**leclairparis.com/**

If you want to party and have a proper drink in the 7th arrondissement, L'Eclair is your best choice. This bohemian chic stop on the rue Cler complete with a cozy terrace, is open for breakfast, lunch, and dinner, but the surprise is the intellect behind the bar. Yes, they offer some sweeter stuff for cocktail newbies, but Sulyman the barman is making his own bitters, curing his own rum, and taking his job seriously. His spin on the cucumber martini is perfection, and for something a bit sweeter but still balanced, try the Porn Star Martini with passion fruit and a shot of Champagne! Hopefully, it's the only time you and this phrase are mentioned in the same sentence.

"IF YOU ASK THE GREAT CITY, 'WHO IS THIS PERSON?,' SHE WILL ANSWER, 'HE IS MY CHILD.'"

*Victor Hugo, Les Misérables*

# — LA SAUVAGE BEE'S KNEES —

Treize co-owner, Kajsa von Sydow, created this cocktail for the Josephine en Rose Celebration at the Casino de Paris, held by Maison Noir Americaine, for Josephine Baker's move to the Pantheon in 2021.

---

- **1¾ oz. spiced honey infused gin**
- **1 oz. freshly squeezed and strained lime juice**
- **½ oz. honey syrup**
- **¾ oz. Giffard banana liqueur**
- **1 egg white**

---

**METHOD:** Add all ingredients to a shaker and dry shake (without ice) for several seconds. Fill shake ½ full of ice and shake vigorously before pouring into a chilled Champagne coupe. Garnish with a lemon zest and drop in a cocktail cherry.

"I use Hendricks cucumber infused gin, for a touch of that crispy freshness, and then I infuse it with Treize Chef Laurel's spice-infused-honey, with notes of ginger, cinnamon, and nuts; balanced with fresh lime juice, and a touch of banana liquor. Served with a maraschino cherry, for that appropriate decadent ending."

+++

**Kajsa von Sydow**

## Raphael Terrace

**17 Avenue Kléber, 75116 Paris**
**Phone: 01 53 64 32 00**
**Price:** ***
**Atmosphere: Inviting**
**raphael-hotel.com/**

Hiding inside this somewhat staid hotel are two secrets. First, downstairs in the English gentleman's bar, which has been virtually untouched since the opening of the hotel in 1924, you'll find the spot where the late French singer and cultural icon Serge Gainsberg spent his nights drinking Gibsons. Upstairs, in fine weather, call ahead and book a table with a bottle of Champagne or wrestle through the crowd to get a much-coveted seat on the roof with a view of all of Paris. Yes, it's worth the fight, and once settled, Christian Gomez, the chef du bar, will treat you like you belong.

# — RAPHAEL —

This signature drink at the rooftop bar at the Raphael hotel is fresh and breezy.

- **2 oz. strawberry puree**
- **½ oz. Manzana Verde**
- **1 tablespoon fresh lime juice**
- **Brut Champagne to top**

**METHOD:** Shake strawberry puree, Manzana Verde, and lime juice together together into a cocktail shaker with ice, and strain.

**SERVING SUGGESTION:** Serve in a chilled Champagne glass, topping off with Brut Champagne. Garnish with a strawberry.

> Manzana Verde is a green apple liqueur made by a number of companies, including Briottet and Giffard, which are good French brands.

# — EN PLEIN AIR —

ICED TEA PEYI 64

LA ZEZETTE 69

BISOUS DU SOLEIL 70

ROSE DE VARSOVIE 73

Drinking outdoors in Paris is magical. To prendre un verre and indulge in some people watching, or view-goggling, is a pastime that is taken seriously in all seasons by Parisians and visitors alike. The following drinks are the perfect way to transport you to a Parisian terrace or French outdoor adventure.

# — ICED TEA PEYI —

Imagine you are on a sailboat sailing around Martinique when you sip this one, coming to us via Michael at Maria Loca (page 218).

- **1½ oz. White Agricole Rhum or Cachaça Prata (or your favorite rum)**
- **1¾ oz. hibiscus water or agua de Jamaica**
- **2 teaspoons Gomme syrup (or simple syrup)**
- **1 tablespoon lime juice**
- **1 tablespoon Velvet Falernum**
- **1 dash Peychaud bitters**

**METHOD:** Put all ingredients in a cocktail shaker with ice, shake, and serve on ice in a rocks glass.

**SERVING SUGGESTION:** Garnish with a round of lime.

Gomme syrup is slightly different than regular simple syrup and can be purchased, but feel free to substitute simple syrup here.

"FOR ART TO EXIST, FOR ANY SORT OF AESTHETIC ACTIVITY OR PERCEPTION TO EXIST, A CERTAIN PHYSIOLOGICAL PRECONDITION IS INDISPENSABLE: INTOXICATION."

*Friedrich Nietzsche*

# *Provençal Party*

The setting must be the countryside. It is preferable to set out a long wooden table and cover it with a sweet country tablecloth, something clean but not too fancy. Don't make the mistake of using your patio furniture; it is simply not the same.

Bring out mismatched cups and glasses and napkins. An old pitcher of flowers you've picked will make a delightful centerpiece.

After some drinks and some nibbles, take naps on old blankets in the summer sunshine.

**SERVE:**

**Pastis** is *the* drink in the South of France; the anise-flavoured aperitif (see photo on the opposite page), is normally served on ice, then water is added. The taste of licorice is very refreshing on a sunny day. However some of your guests may prefer a **Bisous du Soleil** (page 70) or a **Rose de Varsovie** (page 73).

**NIBBLES:**

Lay out both **salmon pâté** and a **country pâté** and cut up some **baguette** (the French never serve crackers with pâté so you shouldn't either). Make sure to have a good bowl of olives available such as Lucques. **Crudités** with aioli dipping sauce will strike the right note. After a few cocktails, resort to rosé wine to turn it down a notch. If you wish to serve a proper lunch, several varieties of quiche with a big green salad will work well.

"I like The Eiffel
Tower because it
looks like steel
and lace."

*Natalie Lloyd*

# — LA ZÉZETTE —

As a gastronomy and historical guide, Allison Zinder's Paris research regularly turns up interesting facts. This is how she discovered a little known turn of the century lady's drink with a cheeky name: La Zézette is a children's word for "lady parts."

---

- **1 part absinthe**
- **7 parts sweet, very cold white wine (Sauternes, Montbazillac, Côteaux du Layon, or any other unctuous white wine)**

---

**METHOD:** Pour ingredients into a pitcher and stir. Serve over ice in small glasses.

# — BISOUS DU SOLEIL —

Fruity but not too sweet, perfect for sipping on a sunny day in the French countryside. Created by Krystal Kenney, Paris.

---

- **1 oz. vodka**
- **Dash of Cointreau (or your preferred triple sec)**
- **1½ oz. cranberry juice**
- **Juice of ½ lime**
- **Juice from 1 orange wedge**
- **Add a twist of orange**
- **Fill with Champagne**

---

**METHOD:** Combine vodka, Cointreau, and the juices in a cocktail shaker with ice. Shake and strain.

**SERVING SUGGESTION:** Serve in a coupe glass with a twist of orange and top off with Champagne.

> A coupe glass is an old-fashioned Champagne glass in the shape of Marie Antoinette's breasts—an old wives' tale but a good one.

## Al Fresco Views Worth Drinking To

### Hôtel Particulier Bar

**23 Avenue Junot, Pavillon D, 75018 Paris**
**Phone: 01 53 41 81 40**
**Price: *****
**Atmosphere: Secret garden**
**hotel-particulier-montmartre.com/**

Hidden down a little path next to a petanque court in the rear of the Hôtel Particulier, is a secret little outdoor haven for drinks in the summer behind the hotel of the same name. A more romantic spot cannot be found. Read the directions carefully on the website, or you'll never find this little gem. If you want to have an illicit affair, this is the spot; there are even hotel rooms upstairs should the mood be right.

### Le Tout-Paris

**8 Quai du Louvre 75001 Paris**
**Phone: 01 79 35 50 22**
**Price: *****
**Atmosphere: Très Parisian**
**letoutparis.fr**

For one of the best views in Paris, grab a seat on the rooftop terrace of this newly opened brasserie and bar with a front row view of the Seine and the charming city center. The rooftop restaurant and bar are part of the Cheval Blanc hotel that's housed in the newly re-opened Samaritan. This was one of the most anticipated reopenings of the last decade and location, view and cocktails were all worth the wait! The bar has also created "mirror" versions of many of their cocktail creations that are alcohol free, but still delicious.

### Le Perchoir

**14 rue Crespin du Gast, 75011 Paris**
**Phone: 01 48 06 18 48**
**Price: ****
**Atmosphere: Aerial**
**leperchoir.fr**

Le Perchoir helped usher in a new kind of rooftop Paris bar. While previously most of the rooftop bars were in high-end hotels, this young and trendy venue created a more vibrant and laid back space and ambience. This is where to go for fun and refreshing drinks, DJs, and people-watching. Thanks to the popularity of the original, a handful of sister Perchoirs are now dotted around Paris for even more rooftop views.

# — ROSE DE VARSOVIE —

Though the historic Bar le Forvm may have closed, we can still appreciate its spirit through the many cocktails created by its talented team over the years. This ladylike drink is perfect for a summertime lunch in your garden.

---

- **1¾ oz. vodka**
- **½ oz. Peter Heering Cherry liqueur**
- **4 drops de Cointreau (or your preferred triple sec)**
- **3–4 drops of Angostura bitters**

---

**METHOD:** Place all ingredients in a glass and stir with ice for about 15 seconds.

Strain into frozen martini glass.

**SERVING SUGGESTION:** Garnish with a cocktail cherry.

# DU VIN

KIR ST. LOUIS 78

ROSÉ-PAMP 79

VERDANT MARTINI 81

SHERRY CHERIE 83

THE BASTILLE CELEBRATION 86

SERENDIPITI 87

DEATH IN THE AFTERNOON 88

A traditional apéritif in France has *toujours* been *un verre de Champagne.* True, it's hard to go wrong ordering that, but due to the country's love for wine and Champagne, there is an inordinate amount of superb recipes presented in Paris bars using Champagne and other wines to "top off" a cocktail, making the drink a sparkling adventure.

One would be remiss not mentioning an important part of the Parisian drinking scene: wine bars. They've been around forever, but wine bars serving uniquely (or a least some) natural wine has been the craze for almost a decade now.

Wine bars are a great way to start, end, or pass a night out (or in!) when you need a little break from your cocktails. But you can always combine the best of both worlds with wine or Champagne cocktails!

"CHAMPAGNE IS ONE OF THE ELEGANT EXTRAS IN LIFE."

—*Charles Dickens*

## — KIR ST. LOUIS —

This twist on the Kir was created by friends at my apartment on the Ile St. Louis.

- **½ oz. St-Germain (or other elderflower liqueur)**
- **1 oz. Pamplemousse Rose liqueur**
- **Champagne to fill**

**METHOD:** Pour elderflower liqueur and Pamplemousse in a Champagne glass, and top with Champagne.

**SERVING SUGGESTION:** Serve in a Champagne glass with a horse's neck grapefruit rind.

> A horse neck twist is created by cutting the citrus (lemon, grapefruit, or lime) with a sharp pairing knife around in a circle while spinning the fruit to create a long spiral.

# — ROSÉ-PAMP —

A perfect summery cocktail for a shady spot on a summer day.

- **1 oz. Pink Grapefruit Liqueur (Edmond Briottet grapefruit liqueur is a good brand)**
- **4 oz. cold rosé wine**

**METHOD:** Combine the liqueur and wine and serve in a chilled wine glass.

*Le plus lourd fardeau, c'est d'exister sans vivre.*

THE GREATEST BURDEN IS TO EXIST WITHOUT LIVING.

—VICTOR HUGO

# — VERDANT MARTINI —

The in-the-know crowd saunters into the bar of L'Apicius restaurant for pre-dinner drinks or leisurely, luxurious bespoke cocktails. Former bartender, Valentin Calvel, created this stunning martini variation that mirrors the verdant scenery in their gorgeous summer garden terrace..

---

- **4 green shiso cress**
- **2 borage cress**
- **Kona Sansho (Japanese pepper)**
- **2 oz. London dry gin (or your favorite gin)**
- **2 dashes Noilly prat dry vermouth**

---

**METHOD:** In a mixing glass, add green shiso, borage, a pinch of Kona Sansho, gin, Noilly Prat and a lot of ice. Stir aggressively. Double strain into a very cold martini glass.

**SERVING SUGGESTION:** Decorate with a green shiso, purple shiso, and borage cress leaves.

**VARIATION:** Replace the gin with your favorite vodka.

> To make this particularly elegant and exotic martini as Valentin does in Paris, you'll want to visit an Asian market for some of the more unusual products such as the Japanese pepper, which comes in a bottle (Kona Sancho), and the shiso leaves. The borage cress are the first sprout leaves of a borage plant and taste like cucumber. If you can't find the cress, substitute a thin slice of a Japanese or European cucumber.

## — SHERRY CHERIE —

Created by Jen Riley at the Red House, this unique Champagne cocktail has French and Portuguese elements plus a hint of the tropics.

- **1½ oz. Amontillado Sherry**
- **1 tablespoon dry curaçao, preferably Pierre Ferrand (or your favorite orange-flavored liqueur)**
- **2 teaspoons simple syrup**
- **1 oz. tamarind water**
- **Chilled dry Champagne to top**

**METHOD:** Build this cocktail straight into a highball style glass over ice, stir, and top off with Champagne.

**SERVING SUGGESTION:** Garnish with a sprig of rosemary.

> Tamarind is a sweet and sour fruit found in Southeast Asia. Buying tamarind paste is quite easy online or at an Indian or Asian market. Use 2 teaspoons of the paste with ¾ cup of hot water to dissolve. Cool down and strain before using. The closest substitute for tamarind water would be diluted lime juice, but it won't be quite the same.

# *Sparkling Fête*

This is a French-themed artsy party that is perfect to celebrate an engagement, the birth of a baby, a big birthday party, or even New Year's!

Buy a gigantic piece of poster board, or better yet, stretch and temporarily pin some canvas across a blank wall. Provide a set of pastels and charcoal. After handing a guest one of the Champagne cocktails you have on offer, ask them to draw some good wishes for the happy couple, the New Year, or whatever you are celebrating. This can be given to the person(s) of honor as a parting gift.

**SERVE:**

- A whiskey-based Champagne cocktail, the Bastille Celebration (page 86)
- The Serendipiti, made with Calvados (page 87)
- The absinthe-kissed Death in the Afternoon (page 88)

**NIBBLES:**

**FRENCH HERB DIP** served in a half of a red pepper with crudités. To make the herb dip: Combine a soft goat cheese with fresh herbs (like chervil, parsley, chives and tarragon), add herbes de Provence, yogurt, sour cream, and lemon zest until consistency and flavor is just right.

**OYSTERS ON THE HALF-SHELL** (from Normandy if you can get them). Serve with a *piment d'espelette* sauce:

- 1 tablespoon finely chopped shallot
- 2 teaspoons fresh lemon juice
- 2 teaspoons white wine wine vinegar
- 1 cup mayonnaise
- 1 teaspoon piment d'Espelette
- Coarse sea salt
- Freshly ground black pepper

- Salmon rillettes (make or buy)
- Escargot with warm crusty bread
- A superb selection of French chocolates, or make your own Cognac truffles

# — THE BASTILLE CELEBRATION —

Does your evening call for a celebration? This lovely concoction should do the trick.

- **2 oz. Bastille Whisky**
- **A splash of St-Germain (or other elderflower liqueur)**
- **Champagne**

**METHOD:** In a chilled Champagne glass, combine the whisky and liqueur, and then fill with Champagne.

**SERVING SUGGESTION:** Garnish with a raspberry or a strawberry.

> This is an easy drink for someone who doesn't know that they like whisky… yet.

# — SERENDIPITI —

Colin Peter Field, chef du bar at the Ritz, says this is his favorite drink.

- **1 oz. Calvados (or your apple brandy of choice)**
- **A sprig of mint**
- **1 oz. apple juice**
- **Champagne to fill**

**METHOD:** Put apple brandy in a tumbler with the mint and muddle the two ingredients together, slightly bruising the mint.

Add plenty of ice and then the apple juice.

**SERVING SUGGESTION:** Top to the brim with Champagne. Taste, and say *Serendipiti!*

"COME QUICKLY, I AM TASTING THE STARS!"

*Dom Perignon*

# — DEATH IN THE AFTERNOON —

This drink was created by Ernest Hemingway, a man who knew a lot about both Paris and alcohol. Modern day adaptations tone down the absinthe from Papa's original version and make for a celebration-worthy Champagne-based cocktail.

---

- **$^1/_4$ to $^1/_2$ oz. absinthe (to taste)**
- **Champagne**

---

**METHOD:** Pour the absinthe into a chilled flute or coupe and top with Champagne.

**SERVING SUGGESTION:** Add a dash or two of simple syrup for a slightly sweeter version.

"REMEMBER GENTLEMAN, IT'S NOT JUST FRANCE WE'RE FIGHTING FOR, IT'S CHAMPAGNE!"

—*Sir Winston Churchill*

DEPUIS 910
PRODUIT DE FRANCE
ACON VILLAGES
JULIEN GUILLOT
EURL DES VIGNES DU MAYNES
AGRICULTURE FRANCE
Les Débonnaires
CHINON
APPELLATION CHINON CONTROLÉE
vin de france
PRODUCT OF FRANCE

# Wine Bars

## Chez Nous

**10 Rue Dauphine, 75006 Paris**
**Phone: 01 43 26 42 69**
**Price: ***
**Atmosphere: Tapas bar**
**cheznousparis.com/**

At this newly opened natural wine bar you'll find Robin, the owner, who is passionate about his wines and who insists on never serving strange, farm-y or funky natural wines that are undrinkable for all but the mesmerized. Have him guide you and give you a tasting of two or three different glasses that are sure to surprise and really impress you. I had a Chinon from 2012 that knocked my socks off.

"CHAMPAGNE IS THE ONLY WINE THAT LEAVES A WOMAN BEAUTIFUL AFTER DRINKING IT."

—*Madame de Pompadour*

## Clown Bar

**114 rue Amelot, 75011 Paris**
**Phone: 01 43 55 87 35**
**Price: ****
**Atmosphere: Sultry**
**clown-bar-paris.fr/**

Brought to you by the expert team from Saturne, one of my favorite restaurants and natural wine bars, Clown Bar offers small bites and natural wines. The tiny bistro is set in an historic site from 1917 with tiles decorating the walls picturing clowns and other artists from the nearby Cirque d'Hiver (winter circus) who used to frequent the place. Follow manager Xavier's suggestions; he won't lead you astray. Their roasted oysters from Normandy served on a broiled bed of leeks with a touch of cream and pear was unctuous and married well with the Chinon from Anjou. A romantic setting and sexy ambiance makes this a must-try spot for special occasions.

## Le Baron Rouge

**1 Rue Théophile Roussel, 75012 Paris**
**Phone: 01 43 43 14 32**
**Price: ***
**Atmosphere: Brimming with life**

This wine bar near the Aligre market is a local favorite, and you can see why when you arrive around 2 p.m. on a weekend and witness the crowd spill out on the street. This might be the most convivial and friendly place in town, and with prices of wine by the glass at a mere 2 to 4 euros, your wallet won't suffer. Weekends are the most popular because, beyond the variety of assiettes on offer (sausage, hams from Corsica, rillettes, and cheese), you'll find a friendly oysterman outside who shucks for the crowd.

## L'Avant Comptoir

**3 Carrefour de l'Odéon, 75006 Paris**
**Phone: 01 44 27 07 97**
**Price: ****
**Atmosphere: Foodie heaven**

An offshoot of nextdoor restaurant le Comptoir, this darling wine bar has a notoriously fabulous selection of French wines and meat-driven small plates. The pocket-sized space gets packed with Parisian wine-loving foodies, bumping elbows and sharing opinions over rillettes and terrines. If meat's not your thing, they have a seafood version just next door as well.

## L'Ebiniste du Vin

**10 Rue Dauphine, 75006 Paris**
**Phone: 01 42 28 80 43**
**Price: ****
**Atmosphere: Intimate cave soirée**
**lebenisteduvin.fr/**

L'Ebiniste du Vin and its sister L'ecaillier du Ebiniste in the 17th are wine bar extraordinaires with 500 wines on offer and more than 30 by the glass. Go early because by 8:30 p.m. this place is jam-packed with thirty- and forty-something's enjoying their wines, charcuterie, fromage, and crudités. Next door, the L'Ecailler serves fish instead of meats and is a bit smaller and slightly less crowded. Run by a husband-and-wife team, this spot is piping hot in this newly trendy part of the 17th arrondissement.

"Champagne and orange juice is a great drink. The orange improves the champagne. The champagne definitely improves the orange."

—*Philip, Duke of Edinburgh*

# Champagne Bars

Champagne always tastes better in Paris so we've got the inside scoop on the best places to go for a coupe! Cynthia Coutu, Paris-based Champagne instructor and guide shares her round up of three recommended Champagne bars:

## Le Dokhans

**117 Rue Lauriston, 75116 Paris**
**33 1 53 65 66 99**
**hotelledokhansparis.com/le-dokhans-bar**
**Open every day from 18-24h.**

This very chic hotel bar–check out the Louis Vuitton elevator - was the first Champagne bar in Paris. The selection is both extensive and expensive.

## L'Afterbulles

**35 Rue de l'Espérance, 75013 Paris**
**33 1 77 35 11 10**
**vinissime.fr**
**Open from 18-21h on Fridays and Saturdays.**

This very cozy bar specializes in grower Champagne and hosts jazz concerts every second Saturday, and Champagne brunches every second Sunday. Reservation required.

## The French Paradox

**(Also known as Canard et Champagne)**
**57 passage des Panoramas, 75002 Paris**
**33 9 83 30 06 86**
**frenchparadox.paris**
**Open from Monday to Sunday from 12h to 14h and from 19h to 22h30.**

This restaurant/bar that only serves duck and Champagne is tucked away in a charming old passage. They feature both an extensive selection of grower Champagne and Grandes Maisons.

**If you're looking for more unique Champagne activities in Paris, Cynthia also hosts private and group tasting events like Bulles et Boules (play pétanque while sipping Champagne), Champagne and Cheese Pairing, Shop and Sip and more, all exclusively focused on Champagne made by women. The calendar of these regular events**

Champagne

BRUT
BRUT

Champagne

# — JAZZ-ERA INSPIRATIONS —

AVIATION 100

FRENCH 75 SQUARED 101

23 JUMP STREET 103

THE CHAMBER G&T 104

MISTINGUETTE 106

THE FRENCH OLD FASHIONED 110

SINGAPORE SLING 113

SEAPEA 114

2 CHEVAUX 115

LÉA D'ASCO 116

BRAMBLE & QUEEN 119

FORVM COCKTAIL 120

THE BASTILLE SOUR 121

THE FRENCH MANHATTAN 122

LE BON CHIC BON GENRE (BCBG) 123

LADY B 124

THE YEAR OF THE FRENCHMAN 126

THE HARRY'S BLOODY MARY RECIPE 128

CHOCO PEAT 129

1789 131

14 JULLIET 132

FRENCH OPEN PIMM'S CUP 134

LE GRAND'S ORIGINAL DRY MARTINI 135

HIGHLAND CREAM 136

FRENCH WHITE NEGRONI 138

PICASSO MARTINI 140

In researching and talking to bartenders across Paris, I learned that, in fact, cocktails have been part of French culture dating back to the 1800s. But it is also true that the first Golden Age of cocktails in Paris occurred not coincidentally at about the same time as Prohibition began in the United States. Unemployed U.S. bartenders wandered over to Europe, ending up in the great hotels of London and Paris and beyond. Many an important cocktail was invented in Paris during this period and, not surprisingly, this was also a time that *beaucoup de* important American artists and writers descended upon the streets of Paris to seek the freedom and tolerance not found in their home country. Enjoy these Jazz Era-inspired cocktails in style.

# — AVIATION —

This drink gets its color and flavor from a French liqueur made from real violets.

- **1½ oz. gin (Citadelle from France or any other fine artisanal gin)**
- **½ oz. fresh lemon juice**
- **2 dashes Crème de Violette (Briottet or Giffard preferred)**
- **½ oz. Maraschino liqueur (Luxardo preferred)**

**METHOD:** Combine all ingredients into a cocktail shaker with ice. Shake and strain into chilled martini glass.

**SERVING SUGGESTION:** Garnish with a Luxardo maraschino cherry or two!

# — FRENCH 75 SQUARED —

An early version of this classic cocktail, French 75, was popularized at Harry's Bar in Paris in the early 20th century (back then just called the "75"). The modern day version of this little drink is drastically different from the original in terms of recipe, but it's still just as popular. We took the current recipe for this drink and added St-Germain to up the French factor.

---

- **2 oz. gin**
- **1 oz. fresh lemon juice**
- **1 teaspoon sugar**
- **1 oz. St-Germain (or any elderflower liqueur)**
- **Champagne**
- **2 cherries for a garnish and a horse's neck lemon peel (a very long curling twist)**

---

**METHOD:** In a shaker combine the gin, lemon juice, sugar, and elderflower liqueur with cracked ice. Strain and serve in an ice-cold coupe glass about $^2/_3$ full, then fill with brut Champagne.

**SERVING SUGGESTION:** Garnish with 2 Luxardo maraschino cherries and a horse's neck lemon peel (page 78).

> This recipe serves two. Never drink the French 75 Squared alone.

BONAL
APÉRITIF - QUINA
des Montagnes de la Grande Chartreuse
St LAURENT-DU-PONT (ISÈRE)
QUINQUINA VIN APÉRITIF
MAISON FONDÉE EN 1865
PRODUIT DE FRANCE

# — 23 JUMP STREET —

A winning recipe created by Joseph Biolatto and Yoan Bonneau for the Trophées du Bar 2012.

- **1¾ oz. Calle 23 reposado**
- **1 tablespoon Bonal Quina**
- **1 tablespoon *Punt e Mes Carpano* (Italian Vermouth)**
- **6–8 dashes of orange bitters (preferably Fee Bros.)**
- **6–8 dashes of Créole bitters by Bitter Truth**

**METHOD:** Put all ingredients into a cocktail shaker with ice, shake, strain, and serve in a chilled martini glass with an orange twist as garnish.

*Je ne veux pas être trop bourré(e).*

I DON'T WANT TO GET TOO DRUNK.

# — THE CHAMBER G&T —

Gin and Tonics have been drunk since the nineteenth century and have carried on throughout time in bars all over the world. "I believe the mojito has had too long of a day in Paris and it's time to replace it with a classic that is fresher and more updated," said its creator, Forest Collins. This recipe stands out thanks to the brands used, which make for a more elegant G&T, and the addition of the edible violet that recalls the botanicals in the French gin. The name is an homage to The Chamber, a former private cocktail social club founded by Ms. Collins where the drink was served.

---

- **1½ oz. Citadelle gin (a French gin)**
- **4½ oz. Fever Tree tonic water**
- **Lemon zest**

---

**METHOD:** Fill chilled jelly jar (or high-ball glass) with ice cubes. Pour one part gin and three parts tonic water into the glass. Express lemon zest over the cocktail, and drop zest into the drink.

**SERVING SUGGESTION:** Garnish with an edible violet.

"Single-handedly I'm trying to get Parisians to start drinking G&Ts as their go-to drink instead of Mojitos."

+++

**Forest Collins, influential cocktail blogger in Paris, 52Martinis.com.**

# — MISTINGUETTE —

This drink's namesake was a famous French actress, singer, and dancer at the turn of the century. Her titillating act at the Moulin Rouge (and other cabarets) made her one of the highest-paid female entertainers in the world. Created by Paris bartender Romain Krot.

---

- **½ oz. honey syrup infused with horseradish**
- **½ oz. pink grapefruit juice**
- **2 teaspoons fresh lemon juice**
- **1 oz. Lillet Blanc**
- **1 oz. vodka**
- **Dash Jamaican jerk bitters**
- **Garnish with grapefruit zest**

---

**METHOD:** Start with the honey syrup infused with horseradish. Make this like you would a simple syrup but instead of sugar substitute honey and then add some grated horseradish, cool, strain, and pour. Shake all ingredients except the grapefruit zest in a cocktail shaker and strain.

**SERVING SUGGESTION:** Serve in a chilled martini glass with grapefruit zest floating on top.

MOULIN ROUGE

# Jazz Era Celebration

Ask your guests to come in their zoot suits, their fedoras, and their flapper dresses. Feathered headgear is welcome, as are long strands of pearls. In the 1920s, Paris was a hotbed of excitement and late nights were had in Montparnasse drinking in the flavors of the moment. Search for some swing and ragtime jazz on iTunes and throw in a little Piaf for good measure to put your guests in the mood.

**SERVE:**

**French Old Fashioned (page 110) • Singapore Slings (page 110) • Forvm Cocktail (page 120)**

**NIBBLES:**

**Simple classic appetizers such as devilish eggs, pork rillettes served with French bread, and devils on horseback (bacon wrapped around prunes and baked).**

After a few cocktails, turn up the music and dance the night away imaging that F. Scott Fitzgerald or Gertrude Stein might just walk in the door any minute.

# — THE FRENCH OLD FASHIONED —

The Old Fashioned was one of the earliest cocktails. Back in the day, cocktails were often considered medicinal and sometimes taken in the morning after having too much the night before. Now, I enjoy an Old Fashioned, but never ever during an hour that ends in a.m.

---

- **2 oz. French whisky**
- **6 dashes Angostura bitters**
- **$^{1}/_{2}$ to 1 teaspoon sugar (to taste)**
- **1 orange twist for garnish**

---

**METHOD:** Combine the bitters and sugar in the bottom of a rocks glass and muddle together to help the sugar dissolve. Add whisky and a large ice cube and stir. Garnish with an orange zest.

**TIP:** you can also replace the sugar with a simple syrup, which means the sugar will dissolve quicker into the drink.

# — SINGAPORE SLING —

The Singapore Sling was first created in Singapore at the Raffles hotel around 1915. It's a pleasure to try this less-sweet version at the Raffles-owned, Phillippe Starck–designed bar at Le Royal Monceau, Paris (page 36).

- **1 oz. gin**
- **1¾ tablespoons of cherry brandy**
- **2 teaspoons Cointreau (or your preferred triple sec)**
- **3 teaspoons Bénédictine**
- **A dash of grenadine**
- **1⅓ tablespoons lime juice**
- **1 oz. pineapple juice**
- **Soda water to fill**

**METHOD:** Put all the ingredients except the soda into the shaker with ice. Shake vigorously and serve in a high-ball glass with ice cubes and top up with soda water.

**SERVING SUGGESTION:** Garnish with three maraschino cherries and a slice of lemon.

*à Votre Santé!*

TO YOUR HEATH!
(THIS IS YOUR MOST STANDARD PHRASE TO USE WHEN TOASTING; IT CAN BE SHORTENED TO À LA VOTRE OR JUST SANTÉ).

# — SEAPEA —

Legend has it that Frank Meier, bartender at the Bar Hemingway in the Paris Ritz Hotel created this to celebrate composer Cole Porter, who was a regular. The name of the cocktail is a nod to his initials "C.P." While the original was rather bracing, we include here the more modern-day version with egg white, which softens the cocktail nicely.

---

- **2 oz. Pasits (such as Pernod)**
- **1 oz. fresh lemon juice**
- **$^{3}/_{4}$ oz. simple syrup**
- **1 egg white**
- **soda water to fill**

---

**METHOD:** Add the pastis, lemon juice, simple syrup and egg white to shaker without ice and shake vigorously for several seconds. Add ice to the shaker and shake vigorously for another 10 seconds. Pour all ingredients into a chilled Collins glass and top with soda water.

# — 2 CHEVAUX —

This cocktail was created by Kate Hill, a culinary professional who writes, mentors, teaches and cooks from her story-book old home in Gascon, Kitchen at Camont. It's a fun take on a Sidecar, swapping out the Cognac for armagnac and named after the legendary vintage French Citroen 2CV (deux-chevaux).

---

- **2 oz. Armagnac**
- **¾ oz. Curaçao**
- **¾ oz. fresh lemon juice**
- **1 teaspoon simple syrup (optional, for extra sweetness)**

---

**METHOD:** Shake with ice, strain into chilled cocktail glass, express orange peel over drink and (optionally) drop in twist as a garnish.

"SOMETHING ABOUT GLAMOUR INTERESTED ME.
ALL MY SCHOOLBOOKS HAD DRAWINGS OF WOMEN ON TERRACES WITH A COCKTAIL AND A CIGARETTE."

—*Bill Blass*

# — LÉA D'ASCO —

Here we have an English and French combo, which is what its creator Matthew Long is: a Londoner who is very much at home behind a bar in France. Long created this drink while working at the Paris bar Lulu White and named it after a singer from the nearby iconic music hall Folies Bergère.

---

- **½ oz. Beefeater Gin**
- **1 oz. Lillet Blanc**
- **1 tablespoon Armorik Classic Whisky from Brittany**
- **A little bit less than 1 tablespoon Pernod Absinthe**
- **Orange zest for garnish**

---

**METHOD:** Stir all liquid ingredients above together for 20 seconds.

**SERVING SUGGESTION:** Strain into a chilled martini glass and garnish with orange zest.

> Absinthe is an alcoholic substance infused with wormwood. Pernod is one of the oldest producers. Absinthe was banned in 1912 in the United States due to a myth that is caused hallucinations. The ban was lifted in 2007. Absinthe is now made in Switzerland (where it originated), France, Germany, the Czech Republic, and the States.

green
Absinthe
BOHEMIA
PICASSO

## — BRAMBLE & QUEEN —

This lovely drink might be considered a ladies' cocktail, but don't tell the guys who will also love it! Created at the Park Hyatt Vendome, Paris.

- **½ oz. gin (they use Beefeater at the Vendome)**
- **½ oz. fresh lemon juice**
- **½ oz. sugar cane syrup**
- **1 teaspoon ylang ylang water**
- **Egg white**
- **Champagne to top**
- **1 tablespoon blackberry liqueur**

**METHOD:** Pour the gin, lemon juice, syrup, and ylang ylang water in the shaker. Shake it well with a little bit of egg white to obtain a frothy mixture. Strain the cocktail into a cold martini or coupe glass and top with Champagne adding the blackberry liqueur at the very end.

**SERVING SUGGESTION:** Garnish the cocktail with a lemongrass loop and 3 fresh blackberries on a bamboo stick.

> If you can't find ylang ylang water, substitute jasmine water made by Fee Brothers, among other companies.

# — FORVM COCKTAIL —

This is the signature cocktail of the Bar Le Forvm, a historic bar that recently closed its door permanently after nearly a century of serving drinks to well-healed Parisians. The bar may be gone but you can still salute its spirit with this martini style cocktail.

- **1½ oz. gin**
- **2 teaspoons Noilly Prat Vermouth**
- **4–5 drops Grand Marnier**

**METHOD:** Stir in a large glass with ice, strain, and pour into a frozen martini glass.

**SERVING SUGGESTION:** Garnish with an orange twist.

> I started work on this book with the belief that I did not like gin. I had refused to budge on this position for twenty years. But, after trying gin cocktails all over Paris, in particular the new Pink Peppercorn Gin distilled in France, I changed my mind entirely. If you are still in the other camp, you can always substitute vodka for gin in these recipes but I would urge you to take a fresh look at gin—you might be pleasantly surprised.

# — THE BASTILLE SOUR —

The Whisky Sour is a quintessential classic, but the twist here is using not only a French-made whisky but adding the floral notes of St-Germain liqueur, also crafted in France.

---

- **2 oz. Bastille Whisky**
- **¾ oz. St-Germain liqueur (or any elderflower liqueur)**
- **Juice of $^{3}/_{4}$ fresh lemon**
- **One egg white**

---

**METHOD:** Put all ingredients together in a cocktail shaker with ice.

**SERVING SUGGESTION:** Serve chilled and frothy in a rocks glass with some ice.

"AYE, BUT TODAY'S RAIN IS TOMORROW'S WHISKY."

—*Scottish proverb*

## — THE FRENCH MANHATTAN —

This is my husband's go-to drink in the winter, French-ified by the addition of whisky made in France.

---

- **2½ oz. Bastille Whisky**
- **¼ oz. sweet vermouth**
- **1 dash Angostura bitters**

---

**METHOD:** Shake the liquid ingredients with ice and strain. Serve chilled in a martini class.

**SERVING SUGGESTION:** Garnish with an orange peel twist and a cherry.

# — LE BON CHIC BON GENRE (BCBG) —

Who are the BCBG crowd anyway? These are your French preppies; you'll find them in the 16th and 7th arrondissements in Paris. They can be easily spotted wearing cashmere sweaters in bright colors wrapped around their shoulders. But even if this type doesn't appeal to you, this drink will.

---

- **Muddled fresh rosemary, orange zest, and agave nectar**
- **2 oz. Bastille Whisky**
- **2 oz. Domaine de Canton (or any ginger liqueur)**
- **1 oz. white wine**
- **2 oz. apple cider**
- **Splash of fresh lemon juice**

---

**METHOD:** Muddle your herbs, orange zest, and agave nectar; add the rest of the ingredients and shake with ice. Strain, and serve on the rocks in a highball glass.

**SERVING SUGGESTION:** Garnish with a sprig of rosemary.

> Domaine de Canton is a ginger liqueur produced in Jarnac, France using Cognac and baby Chinese ginger, among other ingredients.

# — LADY B —

If you are trying to introduce a lady to whisky, first of all you must use Brenne, which is aged in Cognac barrels. It's also 100 percent smoother than most whisky I've tasted. With these two additions, you can turn a whisky-hater into a whisky-lover in one cocktail.

---

- **2 oz. Brenne Whisky**
- **2 oz. Lillet**
- **2 oz. soda water**

---

**METHOD:** Stir the whisky and Lillet together with ice and strain over ice into a rocks glass. Top with soda water.

**SERVING SUGGESTION:** Garnish with an orange peel.

LILLET
Established in 1872
LILLET A PODENSAC-GIRON
Apéritif de France
PRODUCED AND BOTTLED BY:
LILLET
Podensac - Gironde - France
PRODUCT OF FRANCE
ERVE WELL CHILLE

## — THE YEAR OF THE FRENCHMAN —

I adore the title of this drink, and knowing it comes from a former American ballerina who now makes Brenne Whisky in the Cognac region of France just makes it all the merrier.

---

- **2 oz. Brenne Whisky**
- **½ oz. agave nectar (or simple syrup)**
- **¾ oz. fresh lime juice**
- **3 dashes celery bitters**
- **1 teaspoon Sorel (or any hibiscus liqueur)**

---

**METHOD:** Shake all ingredients except the hibiscus liqueur with ice and strain into a chilled coupe glass.

Float a teaspoon of Sorel or other hibiscus liqueur on top.

> Sorel is a brand of hibiscus liqueur made by the company Jack from Brooklyn. But several companies make hibiscus liqueurs.

# Historic Bars

## Harry's New York Bar

**5 Daunou Street, 75002 Paris**

**Phone: 01 42 61 71 14**

**Price:** **

**Atmosphere: Classic New York style**

**http://www.harrysbar.fr/**

An institution in the 2nd arrondissement inhabiting the same spot since 1911, this New York Bar was actually moved to Paris over 100 years ago and then later bought by its first bartender named Harry. This place is all about class, great service, and incredibly smooth classic cocktails. The ambiance upstairs and down is heaven, exactly what a New York–style bar should look and feel like. There's jazz downstairs on the weekends, but buyer beware: there's no nonsense around here—Harry's serves absolutely no wine and no coffee—you are coming here to drink, baby!

## — THE HARRY'S BLOODY MARY RECIPE —

Created by Harry's New York Bar in 1921 by bartender Ferdinand "Pete" Petiot to help a regular's hangover, what's noticeable here is what isn't included in later recipes. There's no lime (just lemon), no celery salt, no Tabasco sauce, and no horseradish.

---

- **Salt, cayenne pepper, and black pepper to taste**
- **6 dashes Worstershire sauce**
- **Juice of ½ a lemon**
- **2 oz. vodka**
- **2 oz. tomato juice**

---

**METHOD:** Create this in the glass starting with 4 dashes of salt, 2 of cayenne, and 2 dashed of black pepper.

Add the Worstershire, lemon, vodka, and finally the tomato juice.

> Be sure to use ground not cracked black pepper and do not add celery salt! Originally there was no garnish, and to this day at Harry's you won't get a wedge of lemon, or a celery stick, or, God forbid, a pickle! They do add Tabasco sauce now, so feel free to add a dash or two to this if you prefer, but why not give it a sip first?

# — CHOCO PEAT —

If you like chocolate, you'll love this one! Here's another drink that can convert a non-whisky lover into one. I like to substitute this instead of dessert. Created at Harry's Bar, Paris.

- **½ oz. dark chocolate liqueur (Monin brand is preferred)**
- **¾ oz. Kahlua**
- **1¼ oz. Stolichnaya Hot Vodka (or any spicy vodka)**
- **¾ oz. Peat Monster Whisky**

**METHOD:** Stir all ingredients in a cocktail glass with ice, strain, and serve in a martini glass, no garnish needed.

BONA
APÉRITIF - QUI
des Montagnes de la Grande Cha
QUINQUINA VIN APÉ
DISTILLERIE BO
PRODUIT DE FRANC

# — 1789 —

1789 was the year of the storming of the Bastille, the first French revolution (there were a few, in fact). Created by Harry's Bar, Paris.

---

- **½ oz. Bonal Quina (or your preferred apéritif white wine)**
- **½ oz. Lillet**
- **1 ⅓ oz. Bastille Whisky**

---

**METHOD:** In a mixing glass add all three ingredients with ice cubes, stir, strain, and serve in a chilled martini glass.

**SERVING SUGGESTION:** Rim just half the martini glass with Tabasco salt.

> Bonal Quina and Lillet are both French apéritif wines.

# — 14 JULLIET —

Harry's New York Bar created this as a cocktail to complement the first French whisky they ever served: Bastille (hence the patriotic name).

- **4 lime wedges**
- **2 oz. Bastille Whisky**
- **½ tablespoon fig syrup (Monin makes a good one)**
- **Ginger beer to top**

**METHOD:** Squeeze the lime into a tumbler full of ice, and add whisky and the fig syrup (add less than the allotted amount if you like your drink less sweet). Top off with ginger beer (Fever Tree recommended). Ahhh, refreshing!

> If you'd prefer to make your own fig syrup rather than buying it, take a dozen figs (trimming off tops and bottoms) and add them to your simple syrup as you heat it up. Mash the figs as the water simmers. Take off stove after about 5–10 minutes or once sugar has dissolved; let sit to macerate fully for about 20–30 minutes. Strain and use or place in refrigerator for up to two weeks.

## Bar Hemingway at the Ritz Paris

**15 Place Vendome, 75001 Paris**
**Phone: 01 43 16 30 30**
**Price: *****
**Atmosphere: Stepping back in time**
**ritzparis.com/**

This bar holds a critical place in the history of Paris cocktail culture. *Chef du bar* Colin Peter Field was named by *Forbes* as the greatest bartender in the world. If you read his book *Bar Hemingway,* you might agree. His predecessor Frank Meier, who served Ernest Hemingway among other elites, was also enormously important in developing the cocktails we still drink today. The Sidecar was invented by Frank, but I'd suggest trying the Ritz's Pimm's Cup in the summer (after all, the bartender is British). Or make yourself a French-ified version, a French Open Pimm's Cup (page 134).

## Le Grand Hotel

**2 Rue Scribe, 75009 Paris**
**Phone: 01 40 07 32 32**
**Price: *****
**Atmosphere: Historic and grand**
**ihg.com/intercontinental/hotels/gb/en/paris/parhb/hoteldetail**

It was a grand pleasure to sip their own version of the classic gin martini created by Frank Newman in 1904 in this historic bar that's been at this very location since the hotel was created by Napoleon III. While my go-to martini is made with vodka, olives, and onions, it was exciting to try Le Grand's Original Dry Martini (page 135) with Tanqueray gin, Noilly Prat Vermouth, orange bitters, and a Luxardo maraschino cherry. This bar should be your go-to place for a drink before or after attending the Opera Garnier next door.

"HERE'S TO ALCOHOL, THE ROSE COLORED GLASSES OF LIFE."

*F. Scott Fitzgerald, The Beautiful and Damned*

# — FRENCH OPEN PIMM'S CUP —

The Pimm's Cup is the most English of cocktails invented in the UK is popular at Wimbledon, polo, and cricket matches. Here we French-ify it a bit with Lorina French sparkling lemonade. Make a pitcher for a garden party or an afternoon watching the French Open on the telly.

---

- **2 cups Pimm's No. 1**
- **4 cups Lorina French Sparkling Lemonade**
- **1 English cucumber sliced lengthwise thinly such that everyone can get a slice in their drink**
- **Lemons and limes cut into thin rounds**
- **1 green apple sliced in small edible chunks**
- **8 sprigs of mint crushed**

---

**METHOD:** Begin with a pitcher full of ice and add your fruit, cucumber, and mint stirring a bit to bruise the mint.

Add the Pimm's and the Lorina. Chill before serving.

**SERVING SUGGESTION:** Make sure everyone gets some citrus, apple and mint in their glass as well as more ice.

# — LE GRAND'S ORIGINAL DRY MARTINI —

The "Original Dry Martini," as it was named and created by Frank Newman at the Le Grand hotel bar, is a very different and later version than the classic gin martini that was originally created in New York City. So we can call this the Parisian version, and it is quite tasty although it is anything but dry considering how much vermouth is involved.

---

- **1¼ oz. Noilly Prat dry vermouth**
- **1¼ Tanqueray gin**
- **2 dashes of bitter orange**

---

**METHOD:** Put the ingredients in a mixing glass full of ice and serve in a chilled martini glass without ice cubes.

**SERVING SUGGESTION:** Garnish with a Luxardo maraschino cherry or a basic cocktail cherry.

"I LIKE TO HAVE A MARTINI, TWO AT THE VERY MOST. AFTER THREE I'M UNDER THE TABLE, AFTER FOUR I'M UNDER MY HOST."

*Dorothy Parker*

# — HIGHLAND CREAM —

This is a coffee/choco after-dinner drink with whisky. Colin from Bar Hemingway has been perfecting it for years. I think he's got it right!

---

- **1 oz. Grant's Blended Scotch Whisky**
- **2 oz. coffee liqueur**
- **2 oz. crème de cacao bean liqueur**
- **1 oz. espresso coffee**
- **4 oz. crème fraiche**

---

**METHOD:** Pour all ingredients into a shaker filled with ice.

**SERVING SUGGESTION:** Serve in a Martini glass. Garnish with a little chocolate powder.

"REGULARS ALWAYS COME ALONE AND I OFTEN INTRODUCE WHOMEVER IS THERE TO EACH OTHER UNLESS I NOTICE THAT THEY WANT TO BE ALONE. A BARTENDER MUST BE A SALESMAN AND A HOST."

+++

**COLIN PETER FIELD, HEAD BARTENDER AT THE RITZ AND AUTHOR OF BAR HEMINGWAY**

## Rosebud

**11 B Rue Delambre, 75014 Paris, France**

**Phone: 01 43 35 38 54**

**Price:** **

**Atmosphere: 60s jazz**

Rosebud is an outrageously charming bar in the 14th arrondissement where waiters in white coats serve bone-dry martinis. This circa 1962 bar is Mad Men-meets-Paris where the martini glasses are small and stiff, just as they were back in the day. Only vintage cocktails are on offer such as negronis, fizzes, Collins, and the like. With an older, non-hipster crowd and jazz playing on the speakers, this place is truly my cup of tea, so much so that when I visited I actually ordered a second martini, something I've learned many times that I cannot, should not, and will not ever do again. I'm writing it on the blackboard: *one martini is perfect, two is too much. One martini...*

# — FRENCH WHITE NEGRONI —

A modern day classic with a French touch.

- $1^1/_2$ oz. French gin (such as Citadelle)
- $^1/_2$ oz. Suze
- 1 oz. dry vermouth (French made Noilly Prat or Dolin)
- Orange twist

**METHOD:** Add the ingredients to a rocks glass over several large chunks of ice and stir. Garnish with an orange zest.

**VARIATION:** This drink can also be shaken and strained into a chilled martini glass.

*à Boire ou je tue le chien!*

BRING ME SOMETHING TO DRINK OR I'LL KILL THE DOG (A COLLOQUIALISM).

# — PICASSO MARTINI —

This is a beautiful take on the classic martini via Colin Peter Field from Bar Hemingway at the Ritz. I'll let you discern the Cubist reference.

---

- **Noilly Pratt Vermouth ice cube**
- **Gin or vodka**

---

**METHOD:** Pour your favorite gin or vodka into a frozen martini glass and add the vermouth ice cube.

To make vermouth ice cubes add 2 parts water to 1 part vermouth and freeze in trays. The optimal proportion of vermouth to water will vary slightly depending on the vermouth and the temperature of your freezer so don't hesitate to increase the water if cubes are not as solid as desired.

**SERVING SUGGESTION:** Garnish with olives or lemon twist and, if desired, remove ice cube once martini reaches the optimal level of dryness for your taste. If serving to guests, provide a tiny dish alongside the martini, inviting them to remove as necessary.

"HAPPINESS IS... FINDING TWO OLIVES IN YOUR MARTINI WHEN YOU'RE HUNGRY."

—*Johnny Carson*

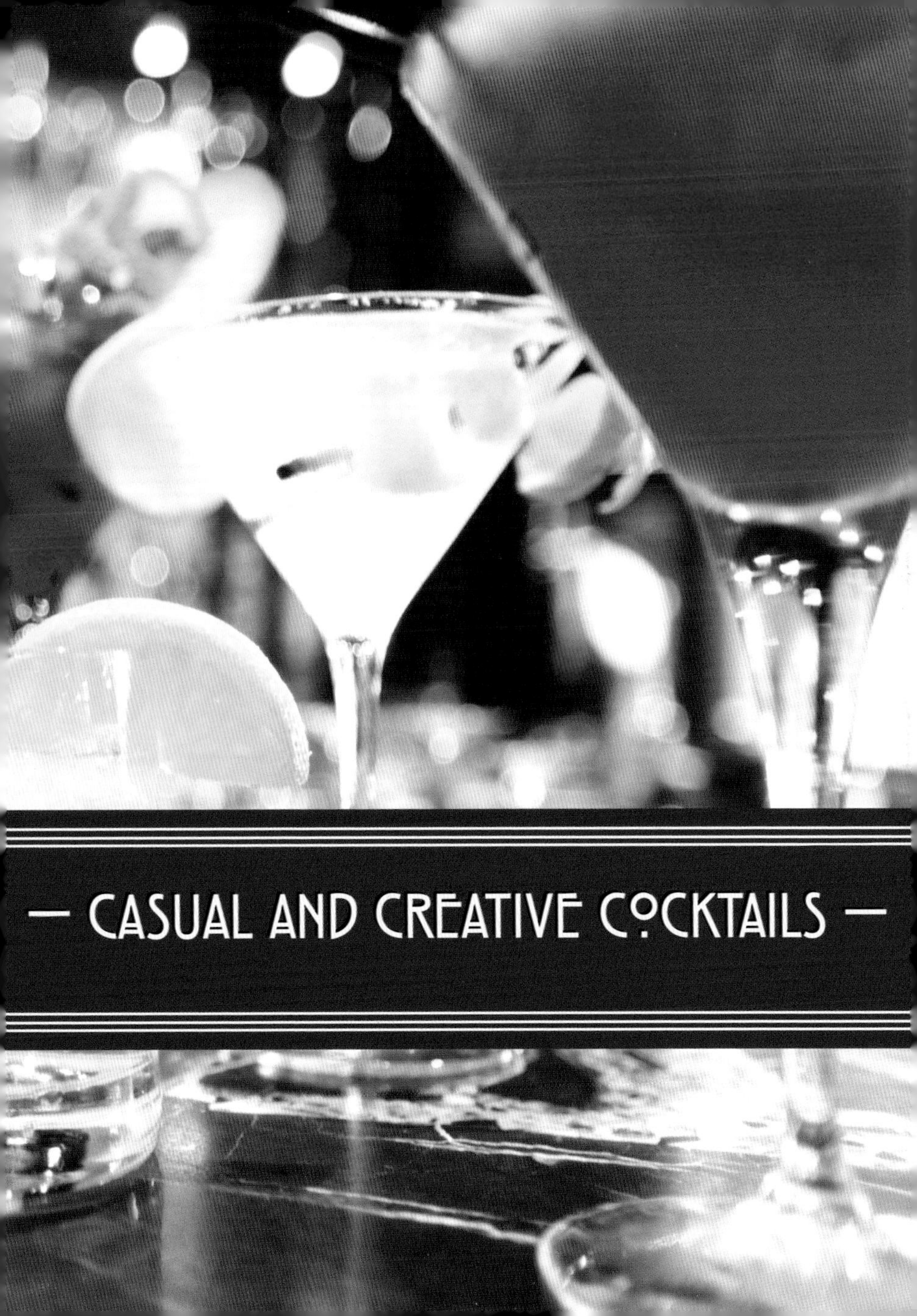

# — CASUAL AND CREATIVE COCKTAILS —

THE SOIRÉE 146

CERISE SOIR 147

L'ORANGE PASSION 150

FRENCH MARTINI DE NANCY 152

CHARLES' JASMINE 153

JENNIFER'S SLIPPER 1544

THE LAST CALL 155

WHITE AGAVE 157

I don't know about you, but I have been in a cocktail rut before. A simple cure for this issue is to step out of your comfort zone. Try an entirely new cocktail from this book to serve to your guests, be they drop-by friends or proper party guests. Perk up a no-plans Friday night creating something entirely new and French-inspired to share with your love. With an open mind and some good products, you'll be surprised at what you can come up with.

Not every night sipping cocktails has to be grand; the new cool-kids casualness that grew up in Brooklyn means that, even when you are not watching your wallet, dive bars—and the drinks those barmen serve—can be a welcome break from having to get your heels and your bowties on. A little down and dirty is good for us all.

*Il n'y a qu'un bonheur dans la vie, c'est d'aimer et d'être aimé.*

THERE IS ONLY ONE HAPPINESS IN LIFE: TO LOVE AND BE LOVED.

(FROM CORRESPONDENCE À LINA CALMATTA BY GEORGES SAND)

# — THE SOIRÉE —

When I was asked to speak about Paris Cocktails for a fête that a friend (the late Patricia Laplante-Collins) was hosting in Paris, I decided to make three cocktails for the group. This was the most successful of them all.

---

- **2 oz. Pink Pepper Gin by Audemus**
- **1 oz. Pamplemousse Rose liqueur (Combier, Cartron & Briottet all make nice versions)**
- **Juice of ½ a lemon**

---

**METHOD:** Stir over ice, pour into a chilled coupe glass, and serve with a lemon twist and several pink peppercorns floating.

**VARIATION:** If you prefer a less strong drink, add Champagne or sparkling water and serve over ice in a tall glass.

> If you can't find the pink peppercorn flavored gin by Audemus, try Big Gin by Captive Spirits made in Seattle or Cardinal Gin made by Southern Artisan spirits of North Carolina.

# — CERISE SOIR —

Created by my friend Jennifer at a Friday night party in Paris, this is a lovely way to enjoy the orange shrubb liquor made in Martinique with rum and orange peel.

- **1 teaspoon simple syrup**
- **Squeeze of a lemon wedge**
- **1 teaspoon Griottines juice (cherries in kirsch)**
- **1 oz. Martinique Shrubb liqueur**

**METHOD:** Shake with ice all ingredients save the cherries, strain, and serve in a cold Nick and Nora glass.

**SERVING SUGGESTION:** Garnish with 2 Griottine cherries (or substitute your favorite cocktail cherries).

> Martinique Shrubb is a liqueur made with rhum agricole and orange. Most of the rhum brands from the island also put out a shrubb, but if you can't find it, you can also look online for recipes for a DIY version.

# —*Make-Your-Own Cocktail Friday*—

This is a casual party; tell your guests to come dressed comfortably. Print out a selection of five to seven of the most intriguing cocktails that you find in this book. Put each recipe (perhaps laminated) in front of a selection of its ingredients at various stations around a large table. Ask everyone to make their own cocktails according to the recipes; tell folks to share tastings to figure out who likes what best.

Lay out a charcuterie *assiette* with a selection of French *fromage*, sausages, pâtés, and Basque hams like jambon de Bayonne. Offer a

spicy espelette pepper jelly alongside some of the harder Spanish or Basque-style cheeses. Include some cherry tomatoes (Parisians are crazy for them!) and French olives, not forgetting a tiny vessel to discard the pits. A big basket of sliced French baguette is *de rigeur*.

For cocktail round two, ask your guests to play around with the ingredients to create their own bespoke concoction.

For the actual meal, serve your favorite soup recipe with more crusty French bread and a bottle or two of Côtes du Rhône.

Follow up the next day by emailing all of your guests the recipes to keep.

## — L'ORANGE PASSION —

This drink was concocted during a drink-making experiment chez moi. It's our French version of a Tequila Sunrise.

---

- **1 oz. tequila**
- **½ oz. Lillet**
- **½ oz. Cointreau (or your preferred triple sec)**
- **Orange juice**
- **Passion fruit juice**
- **Fresh lime juice**

---

**METHOD:** Put the alcohol ingredients above in your cocktail shaker and then add 1 part orange juice and 1 part passion fruit juice (equaling no more than as much as the liquor in the glass for a strong drink and ⅔ to ⅓ liquor for a weaker drink). Add a healthy squeeze of lime. Shake it up well, strain and serve in a highball glass on the rock.

**SERVING SUGGESTION:** Garnish with a lime wedge and lemon peel.

# — FRENCH MARTINI DE NANCY —

One night in Paris, I had a bunch of girls over to make French versions of classic cocktails (hey, a gal can't drink alone, right?) and my friend Nancy, who flew all the way from New York, helped massage this less sweet version of the classic, so she deserves some props.

---

- **½ oz. Pamplemousse Rose liqueur**
- **1½ oz. Ciroc vodka (or your favorite vodka)**
- **A good squeeze of lemon**
- **2 oz. grapefruit juice**
- **Grapefruit zest**

---

**METHOD:** Put the liquid ingredients in your cocktail shaker with ice, shake, and strain.

**SERVING SUGGESTION:** Serve in a martini glass with grapefruit zest sprinkled on top.

# — CHARLES' JASMINE —

Susan Herrmann Loomis, chef, cookbook author, and culinary instructor has made France her home for over two decades. She currently lives in Paris, creating interactive cooking classes for her latest project DancingTomatoes.com. When she entertains at home, this cocktail is her go-to. It's a more easygoing tweak by Charles Malody on the classic Jasmine cocktail.

---

- **$1\frac{1}{3}$ oz. gin**
- **1 oz. bitters**
- **$\frac{3}{4}$ oz. triple sec**
- **1 oz. fresh lemon juice**

---

**METHOD:** Shake all together with ice and strain into a Champagne glass.

*On peut avoir la même chose, s'il vous plaît ?*

ANOTHER ROUND PLEASE!

## — JENNIFER'S SLIPPER —

This recipe comes from the winner of a cocktail contest that we had on the Girls' Guide to Paris Facebook page, and Jennifer won! Interestingly I didn't tell them that they had to use French ingredients, but Midori is actually manufactured in France for all of Europe (though it starts with special melons from Japan).

---

- **1 oz. tequila**
- **½ oz. Midori**
- **2 oz. Sour Mix (see recipe)**

---

**METHOD:** Combine liquid ingredients and shake with crushed ice. Strain, pour, and serve in a frozen martini glass.

**SERVING SUGGESTION:** Garnish with two maraschino cherries.

> **MAKE YOUR OWN SOUR MIX:** Homemade sour mix is much tastier than anything store bought. All you need is: 1 cup sugar, 1 cup water, 2 cups fresh lime and lemon juice strained (no pulp). Combine water and sugar and simmer until the sugar dissolves. Turn the heat down to simmer and add your citrus juice. Remove from the fire and let the mixture sit before straining into a bottle. Store in an airtight bottle in the fridge for up to two weeks. Enjoy!

# — THE LAST CALL —

Not a bad idea to order this up at home as your last call before tucking into bed. Easy to make and smooth on the tongue.

- **2 oz. Brenne Whisky**
- **1 oz. Sorel (Hibiscus Liqueur)**

**METHOD:** Shake the two ingredients with ice and strain into a chilled coupe glass.

**SERVING SUGGESTION:** Garnish with a hibiscus flower.

MIS EN BOUTEILLE AU DOMAINE
Domaine
de Lacave-Barregeat
armagnac
D
42°
ARISTIDE SAMALENS

# — WHITE AGAVE —

Paris-based wine educator and founder of Girl Meets Glass, Tanisha Townsend, suggests borrowing this Chateau Garreau cocktail recipe as a way to enjoy Blanche Armagnac, a more unusual expression of this very French eau de vie.

---

- **1⅓ oz. Blanche Armagnac**
- **⅔ oz. fresh lime juice**
- **⅔ oz. agave syrup**
- **1⅓ oz. sparkling water**

---

**METHOD:** Add Blanche Armagnac, lime juice and agave syrup to shaker filled with ice. Shake and pour into a tall glass filled with ice. Top with sparkling water.

> Blanche Armagnac is not aged in barrels, so it is clear rather than the traditional rich amber or brown color.

## La Folie en Tête

**33 Rue de La Butte aux Cailles, 75013 Paris**
**Phone: 01 45 80 65 99**
**Price: ***
**Atmosphere: Old school artistic**
**lafolieentete.wix.com/lesite**

Looking for a cheap drink in the 13th arrondissement? Then this is your place, especially during happy hour from 5 to 8 p.m. The atmosphere has a relaxed artsy feel, with old school chairs and wooden instruments adorning the walls.

"I wanted to create a neighborhood bar with cheap but good beer and cocktails where it was easy for a young person to be able to buy a round of drinks for their friends. My friend who found the Vespa on the wall has free drinks for life here!"

+++

**Charlotte Galitzine, owner and bartender at Le Charlie**

## Le Charlie

**29 Rue de Cotte, 75012 Paris**
**Phone: 01 53 33 02 67**
**Price: ***
**Atmosphere: Hipster dive**

At the helm is a bartender by the name of Charlotte, who welcomes visitors warmly at her tiny little bar in the Bastille neighborhood. The atmosphere is shabby-hipster dive bar chic, and there's a darling little cave area downstairs where you and your friends can drink all night long. The prices are pleasing.

## Les Pères Populaires

**46 rue de Buzenval, 75020 Paris**
**Phone: 01 43 48 49 22**
**Price: ***
**Atmosphere: Penny-pinching grunge**

If you are looking for the quintessential grunge hipster in Paris, look no further. You'll find hipsters here in droves drinking cheap wine at this unassuming hotspot in the 20th arrondissement. All the wines by the glass come from boxes, but the red Chinon, for a mere 3.5 euros, is quite good. You can order a sandwich or a charcuterie plate and be happy drinking beers or a basic mojito all night long and leave with money left in your pocket.

JOYEUSE HOLIDAYS

PISTE VERTE 164

CHARTREUSE MULE 165

VIN CHAUD 168

CRANBERRY SPARKLER 169

BRENNE CHAI TODDY 170

EDUCATION SENTIMENTALE 172

POMEGRANATE MARGARITA 173

It's truly sublime to spend the holiday season in Paris. One can soak up the spectacle that is Paris and enjoy the season without all the crass commercialization that we now find elsewhere. If you can't make it this year, create your own little French fête at home. *Bonne Année!*

# — PISTE VERTE —

Named after the bunny slope, this winter drink made with pine liqueur is a fresh take on *hiver* by bartender Romain Krot.

---

- **2 teaspoons honey syrup (see instructions below)**
- **1 oz. Mamont Vodka**
- **1 oz. Liqueur de Sapin Dolin**
- **1 oz. fresh clementine juice**
- **½ oz. fresh lemon juice**

---

**METHOD:** Honey syrup is made just like simple syrup but using honey instead of sugar. Heat 1 cup of honey with 1 cup of water until the honey is incorporated and dissolved, let cool, and use. Store the remainder in the fridge for up to 2 weeks.

Shake all ingredients with ice in a cocktail shaker, strain, and serve garnished with mint leaves in a wine glass.

> Sapin liqueur is made in France by a variety of distillers such as Dolin and Les Fils d'Emile Perot.

# — CHARTREUSE MULE —

A take on the Mule using green Chartreuse still made by the Carthusian monks and following a secret centuries old recipe.

---

- **1 oz. Chartreuse Verte**
- **2 teaspoons fresh lemon juice**
- **A splash of ginger beer**

---

**METHOD:** Pour Chartreuse and lemon juice in a rocks glass over ice. Top off with a splash of ginger beer.

*Boire comme un trou*

A COLLOQUIAL PHRASE MEANING TO DRINK A LOT (LITERALLY, DRINK LIKE YOU HAVE A HOLE TO FILL)

## *Joyeuse Noel Fête*

This fête should begin after dinner around 8:30 p.m. because dessert is the concept. Set your iTunes or radio to a playlist of traditional Christmas carols interspersed with some French ones such as those found on the CD "Chants de Noel" (French Christmas Songs) by Hélène Baillargeon.

Offer a selection of French Holiday cocktails such as Vin Chaud (page 168), the Cranberry Sparkler (page 169), and the Brenne Chai Toddy (page 170).

Bring a white elephant gift (something lying around your house that is new and nice but you don't use or care for anymore). You know the drill!

Do a French holiday dessert exchange, similar to a cookie exchange. Ask each guest or couple to bring their favorite French homemade dessert (extra busy souls can buy something spectacular and French at a nearby bakery).

The best type of things to bring to an exchange are items that are small and number at least twenty-five to fifty depending on the number of guests invited. Items such as Cognac truffles, Madeleines, mini-chocolate fondants, macarons, cling-film wrapped slices of Buche de Noel, squares of Nougat blanc, Callissons, Pain des Epices (spicy French Hazelnut Christmas bread), and chocolate-covered orange rind slices.

Supply some nice vintage cookie tins or decorate boxes with tissue. Lay out all of the wares on a table. Nibbling is allowed. Then as people are leaving, have them take several from each offering so that everyone goes home with a nice selection of all of the various desserts. This is the spirit of Christmas: share and share alike.

# — VIN CHAUD —

This classic hot mulled red wine is served in most Parisian bars and cafés all winter long. It will warm you up fast!

- **1 bottle inexpensive red wine (Cote du Rhone or Bordeaux preferred)**
- **1 star anise**
- **2 slices fresh ginger (or sugared ginger)**
- **3 cloves**
- **2 cardamom pods**
- **1 tablespoon of orange and lemon zest**
- **½ cup honey**
- **½ cup Cognac, pear eau de vie, or Calvados (depending on what you like)**

**METHOD:** Put all ingredients except the Cognac into a nonreactive pan with spices, and heat until simmering. Add the Cognac or eau de vie at the end, after you've taken the hot liquid off the fire.

**SERVING SUGGESTION:** Serve in a heat-resistant glass mug with a cinnamon stick.

# — CRANBERRY SPARKLER —

This makes the perfect holiday cocktail.

- **½ oz. Cranberry Liqueur by Edmond Briottet**
- **2 teaspoon of Cocchi Americano Rosa (or sweet vermouth)**
- **2 oz. Champagne (or crémant)**

**METHOD:** Combine the Cranberry Liqueur and Cocchi Rosa in a cocktail shaker with ice. Stir, strain into a chilled Champagne glass, and top off with Champagne or crémant.

**SERVING SUGGESTION:** Float a cranberry or two on top as a garnish.

> Cocchi Rosa is an apéritif-style Italian wine that can be purchased online or at better liquor stores. It's worth seeking out as it has a much better taste in this cocktail than using another sweet vermouth.

## — BRENNE CHAI TODDY —

Similar to the age-old hot toddy, your grandma's cure for a cold, this French version uses a very smooth French whisky aged in Cognac barrels. But then we add Indian spiced chai tea. You won't need a cold to drink this yummy concoction; any chilly day will create the right setting.

---

- **2 oz. Brenne Whisky (an incredibly smooth French-produced whisky)**
- **¼ cup of hot chai tea**
- **½ tablespoon honey**
- **1 cinnamon stick**
- **1 star anise**

---

**METHOD:** Make tea and add honey and let steep. Add the whisky and spices. Sip and enjoy the warmth!

**SERVING SUGGESTION:** Serve with a cinnamon stick and slice of lemon.

## — EDUCATION SENTIMENTALE —

This stunning creation by Jerome of Shake N' Smash uses products from Normandy, where Flaubert, the author of *L'Education Sentimentale,* was from.

---

- **½ oz. homemade chestnut honey syrup (see drink instructions below)**
- **1¾ oz. Christian Drouin Calvados (or any other good Calvados)**
- **½ oz. fresh lemon juice**
- **1 tablespoon Domaine de Canton ginger liqueur or a crushed piece of ginger**
- **A pinch of cinnamon powder**
- **Hard cider**

---

**METHOD:** First, make chestnut honey syrup using an equal amount of honey and hot water infused with chestnuts. Take all the remaining ingredients except the cider and shake in a cocktail shaker with ice.

Strain and serve in a Cognac glass on crushed ice, topping off with the cider. Add more crushed ice so it's nearly overflowing.

**SERVING SUGGESTION:** Garnish with several apple slices standing in the ice.

> At Shake n' Smash, this drink is served with a page from Flaubert's *L'Education Sentimentale* as a coaster.

# — POMEGRANATE MARGARITA —

This would make a very festive holiday season margarita, with a petite French touch.

- **½ oz. Pomegranate Liqueur (Edmond Briottet)**
- **1 oz. Ocho Blanco tequila**
- **1 tablespoon triple sec or Cointreau**
- **2 teaspoons lime juice**

**METHOD:** In a cocktail shaker, shake ingredients with ice, strain, and serve on the rocks in a chilled rocks glass with or without salt and a lime wedge.

**SERVING SUGGESTION:** Float several pomegranate seeds on top.

*Bonne Fête!*

HAPPY HOLIDAY!

(USED FOR A VARIETY OF HOLIDAYS)

# — ARTISANAL COCKTAILS —

CIGARETTE AFTER SEX 181
ZEITOUNI 185
GUEPE VERTE 190
ROSEBUD 191
BLOODY SECRET 193
FALUKA 194
DE LA BRETAGNE 197
EXPÉRIENCE 1 199
OLD CUBAN 201
STEVE CASINO 204
BOBO PARISIEN 206
BLACK POINT À LA FRANÇAISE 207
ROMEO À RIO 209
THE SMOKY SPICY MARGARITA 210
IGGY 215
MOONFLOWER 217
MAZARINETTE 219
RED HOUSE OLD FASHIONED 221
LIBERTINE 222
NIGHT BIRD 223
AUDEMUS CENTURY 224
FUEGO DE COLIMA 229
ESQUISSE NO. 1 230
BURLESQUE 231
LA CONQUISTADOR 233
LE PULPEUX 234
COFFEE OLD FASHIONED 236
FAÇON MARIA 238
LE WOODY WOOD 239

Ready to get creative? The bars and their signature cocktails that I describe in this section are newsworthy ones, the scene setters, the artisanal (craft) bars that have set Paris on fire with excitement. Bartenders in Paris have come from Marseille, Minnesota, London, and beyond to create these unique recipes to thrill Parisians and expat palates alike. Many use homemade, French-made and small batch ingredients in a new, unique way. I paved a path from craft bar to artisan enclave to find the best of the best, presented below. While sometimes you'll need to search beyond your neighborhood liquor store for some ingredients, the fruits of your labors will be rewarded grandly.

> The popular craft bars listed here get very busy at prime hours and on the weekend. Go early evening, midweek or reserve where possible.

You've heard of craft beer but what the heck is a craft bar? How do you know you are in a craft bar as opposed to a regular pub or a fancy cocktail bar? It's all about the ingredients. Whether you are in Paris, New York, or London in a craft bar, you'll find more than ten types of bitters, a variety of fresh herbs, dried and fresh fruits—in other words, much more than your standard line up of lemon and lime wedges. At a craft bar, you'll also notice loads of different types of vermouths and bitter-flavored alcohols and you won't find what is traditionally called *well liquors*, those cheap brands that they automatically reach for when you order a standard drink.

Industrial brands such as Gordon's, Smirnoff, or Seagrams are strictly *verboten* at a craft bar because the word "craft" indicates a predilection for items that are homemade, made in small batches, or made in an artisanal fashion. There has been an effort worldwide on the part the millennial generation to get back to making things by hand, which has led to the rise of craft cocktails and craft bars. Don't be intimidated by the craft cocktail recipes in this chapter—if you can get your hands on the unique ingredients, they're worth making!

> "MY COCKTAIL, IT'S LIKE A PASSPORT FOR THEM, OR A FINGERPRINT—UNIQUE TO JUST THEM. THIS IS WHY I PREFER TO MAKE BESPOKE COCKTAILS AFTER TALKING TO MY GUEST. I LOVE GIVING HIM OR HER SOMETHING ONLY FOR THEM."
>
> +++
>
> VALENTIN CALVEL,
> BARTENDER AT APICIUS

# — CIGARETTE AFTER SEX —

Valentin, the ingenious bartender at Apicius, has found a way to marry East (Yuzu Saki), West (New York Corn Whiskey), and Middle (Antique Sherry from Spain) in one delicious drink!

- **$^3/_4$ oz. Del Maguey Vida Mezcal**
- **$^1/_2$ oz. Elephant Sloe GIn**
- **$^1/_3$ oz. Verjus**
- **$2^3/_4$ oz. Agua de Jamaica**

**METHOD:** Fill a glass of wine with ice, pour all ingredients over and stir.

**SUGGESTION:** Rim the wine glass with Lapsang Tarim / Souchong before building the drink in it

**TO MAKE AGUA DE JAMAICA:** combine 48g hibiscus and 42g flower honey in 500ml water and mix well.

# An Artisianal Drinks Tasting Party

Invite your most adventurous friends for this very worldly craft cocktail and hors d'oeuvres pairing. Send out your invitations several weeks before this special cocktail party to allow yourself time to source all of the ingredients required, as well as the time to infuse the gin and make any other special ingredients required. Bon appetit!

Pick three of the more challenging recipes in this book, those that require you to make an ingredient ahead of time. Examples include the Alchimia Cocktail, and Oh My Dog.

**Serve:**

- **Alchimia Cocktail (page 37) brings Southeast Asian flair for vodka lovers**
- **Oh My Dog (page 50) hints of a certain kind of proper Englishness**

**Nibbles:**

- **Alongside each drink, serve an appropriate appetizer that will evoke the mood and flavor of each cocktail such as Vietnamese spring rolls with the Alchimia cocktail, guacamole and corn chips with the Swizzle, and smoked salmon canapés with Oh My Dog.**

- **For canapés simply spread some cream cheese (or *fromage frais*) onto a diagonally sliced English cucumber. Top with small slice of smoked salmon about the same size as the cucumber and garnish with a frond of dill. Make enough to serve several to each guest.**

Set out your serving plates of appetizers and give each person one small appetizer plate so that they may sample each of the items. Likewise give each person three *petit* glasses such as sherry glasses. Allow them to try each cocktail with the accompanying appetizer pairing. If you choose the three cocktails above, start with the vodka and then move to gin and finally tequila. Like wine, you'll want to taste from the lighter to the more complex. And, of course, have fun!

## ANDY WAHLOO

**69 Rue Gravilliers, 75003 Paris**
**Phone: 01 42 71 20 38**
**Price:** **
**Atmosphere: Moroccan hipster**
**andywahloo-bar.com/**

Kaled Derouiche is as passionate and knowledgeable about the art of cocktails as anyone you'll meet. His Zeitouni, made with vodka citron, lemongrass, olive oil, and pineapple is a refreshing long drink reminiscent of a warm night in Morocco. His Lorena Forever is a rum-based wonder named after the female distiller of the Zapata rum used in the cocktail. He'll surprise you with drinks made with dry ice and the smell of rosewater on the side for the fun of it, but these details are not just for show. His concoctions are enticing.

"IF YOU COME TO MY BAR TO DRINK BEER OR SPEND 1000 EUROS, I WANT YOU TO BE ABLE TO HAVE THE SAME EXPERIENCE—TO BE ABLE TO HAVE A GOOD COCKTAIL AND FORGET EVERYTHING AND JUST ENJOY."

+++

KALED DEROUICHE
FROM ANDY WAHLOO

## — ZEITOUNI —

From the creative mind of Kaled Derouiche, chief bartender at Andy Wahloo. This drink is meant to evoke an afternoon in Morocco, the place from which Andy Wahloo and their neighboring resto, Derriere, draw their influence.

---

- **4 basil leaves**
- **1 round of fresh pineapple**
- **Several slices Granny Smith apple**
- **2 teapoons simple syrup**
- **1 pinch black pepper**
- **1 pinch salt**
- **2 oz. Ketel One Citroën**
- **1 teaspoon olive oil**

---

**METHOD:** Crush the basil leaves with crushed ice in a cocktail shaker and add the simple syrup. Add the pineapple and Granny Smith apple and mash until juiced. Pour Ketel One and the olive oil into the mixture. Finish with a pinch of salt and pepper. Add ice and shake vigorously. Strain carefully and serve in a chilled coupe glass.

**SERVING SUGGESTION:** Garnish with a dried basil leaf (you may substitute fresh).

## A la Française

**50 rue Léon Frot 75011 Paris**
**Phone: 09 82 49 02 69**
**Price: ****
**Atmosphere: 100% bar française**

Head directly downstairs to the 70s-style drinking den. Chef du bar Stephen Miller is a historian of everything associated with French cocktail culture and products. He has virtually the only 100% French and Francophone bar stocked only with French products of which there is an amazing array. He serves up French cocktails that he's sourced back to the 1800s, and he is as passionate about the topic as anyone in the world. This is a cool craft bar, no doubt, but the interest here is for serious cocktail geeks and passionate Francophiles. This is *the* place to try some impossible-to-find French whiskies, vodkas, gins, and many more France products made in France. Santé!

## Bluebird

**12 Rue Saint-Bernard, 75011 Paris**
**Price: ****
**Ambience: Laidback lounge from a different place and time**

Bluebird is a Liquid Corp creation, which has a rep for fun spots with groovy vibes (like Dirty Dick and Moonshiner). Here the ambience is Californian mid-century modern and the bar makes you feel like you've stepped back in time. Gin lovers take note: they have an especially large selection of your favorite juniper forward spirit. So slip into this comfortable neighborhood hangout with its low light and laidback staff to chill with a gin martini as you contemplate the colorful fish in the centerpiece aquarium. But if that's not your spirit, they've got a fully stocked back bar and the skills to make classics or creations with style.

SPOKE

Dickel

## Café Moderne

**19 Rue Keller, 75011 Paris**
**Phone: 01 47 00 53 62**
**Price: ****
**Atmosphere: Late-night bistro**
**cafemoderne-tbmb.com/**

Charming with an *oh-so-French* atmosphere complete with old French signs and a long wooden bar, these are the hallmarks of a classic French bar and bistro. Yet this place is modern in more than name only. They serve bang-up cocktails made by Mido, who was recently named the best bartender in France, and a menu of items that have been hashed, cut, or ground-up, such as meatballs, tartares, and burgers. Their burgers are damn good, as are their deliciously icy Londoner cocktail, similar to a mint julep but made with gin.

*Ça s'arrose!*

THAT DESERVES A DRINK!

## Candelaria

**52 Rue de Saintonge, 75003 Paris**
**Phone: 01 42 74 41 28**
**Price: ****
**Atmosphere: Bubbling**
**candelariaparis.com/**

You must be in the know to get in here; there is no sign, just a door at the back of a tiny little taco shack in the Marais. Once you walk through the door you'll be treated to scrumptious cocktails and a really vibrant scene. It's famous and it gets crowded so go early or late or on a weeknight and order a Saintonge Sprinz in summer or a Guêpe Verte in winter... *santé!*

# — GUÊPE VERTE —

This cocktail was invented in one of the city's early craft cocktail bars, Candelaria. This spicy tequila concoction inspired local bars to create similar drinks and has become somewhat of a modern day classic.

---

- **1¾ oz. chile infused tequila***
- **1 tablespoon fresh lime juice**
- **1 tablespoon agave nectar**
- **12 cilantro leaves**
- **3 cucumber slices (more for garnish)**

---

**METHOD:** Muddle cucumber, cilantro leaves and lime juice in a shaker. Add tequila, agave nectar and ice. Shake and strain over ice in a rocks glass. Garnish with additional cucumber slices.

***CHILE-INFUSED TEQUILA:** Combine 1.5 cups tequila with 1 jalapeno cut in four. Infuse for 8 hours. Remove chili and use (note: this makes enough for multiple drinks and keeps for many months)

# — ROSEBUD —

A glittering cocktail created and served at Bespoke.

- ¼ oz. Hendrick's gin
- ½ tablespoon Reserva Carlos Alberto sweet vermouth
- ½ oz. Combier crème de rose
- ½ oz. housemade sugarcane syrup (but you can use one that you bought in any local store)
- ½ oz. fresh lemon juice
- 2 dashes cranberry bitters
- Fever Tree tonic water water (or other premium tonic)

**METHOD:** Take a shaker, pour in all the ingredients but the tonic water, shake vigorously, strain into a Collins glass full of ice cubes, and top with the tonic water.

**SERVING SUGGESTION:** Garnish with a rosebud.

*Poisson sans boisson—*
*c'est poison!*

(TO EAT) FISH WITHOUT DRINKING WINE IS POISON.

(THIS IS ALSO A TONGUE TWISTER.)

## Castor Club

**14 Rue Hautefeuille, 75006 Paris**
**Phone: 09 50 64 99 38**
**Price: ****
**Atmosphere: Upscale log cabin**

I never thought I would want to spend time in a Tennessee cabin in Paris until I walked into this darling little bar in the 6th arrondissement. Try the John's Last Word with absinthe and celery juice for something unusual and terribly tasty.

## Combat

**63 Rue de Belleville, 75019 Paris**
**+ 33 (0)9 80 84 78 60**
**Price: ****
**Atmosphere: Working class hipster**
**facebook.com/CombatBelleville/**

Owned by Margot Lecarpentier, one of the city's most influential bartenders, Combat consistently turns out excellent cocktails. Margot conceived of the space as a cocktail bistro with a light, bright and airy ambience. The name comes from both the historical name for the block on which the bar sits as well the ongoing feminist struggle. Combat is an aggressively welcoming and all inclusive bar that turns out damn fine drinks. Try the Combat margarita which includes a touch of both sake and CBD. This addition definitely perks things up in the lesser explored Belleville neighborhood.

## CopperBay

**5 Rue Bouchardon, 75010 Paris**
**Price: ****
**Atmosphere: Bright nautical**
**copperbay.fr/**

This crisp, clean, bright nautically themed bar is owned by three friends, two of whom happen to be women. I'm always happy when I see women taking the helm behind the bar, and this experience was no different. Julien from Montpellier, Aurélie from Bretagne, and Elfi from Avignon greet you with extraordinary and atypical French kindness upon entry. Every season they select a group of classic cocktails to highlight such as sours or Collins or spritzes. They also will have six hand-crafted cocktails that highlight the season. I loved the Piss Pepe, served to me on a cold winter night. This was a hot toddy made with rum and honey laced with evergreens and served with a burning mini pinecone on top.

## — BLOODY SECRET —

A tequila-oriented version of the Bloody Mary served with style by the ladies and gents at CopperBay in Paris.

- **1⅓ oz. tequila**
- **¾ oz. fresh lemon juice**
- **½ tablespoon of Magic Copper Bay potion, which consists of Worcestershire, Tabasco, jalapeño, BBQ spices, Cajun spices, horseradish, and smoked paprika according to your taste**
- **6 dashes roasted garlic bitters**
- **Serve with a small bottle of very high quality tomato juice (Granny's secret brand is preferred)**

**METHOD:** Make this cocktail directly in the high-ball glass with 4 large cubes of ice, adding ingredients and stirring in the order they are shown. If you are able to find a very high-quality tomato juice in a small bottle, serve it on the side and let the recipient pour it in; if not, serve what you have in a small pitcher on the side to pour.

**SERVING SUGGESTION:** Garnish with 2 bay leaves, 1 pickled shallot, and 2 small dried red peppers.

# — FALUKA —

A Faluka is a type of sailing boat used on the Nile. This drink created at CopperBay will let you sail away to foreign lands.

- **1¾ oz. pisco**
- **⅓ oz. fresh lime juice**
- **½ oz. Jellab (combination of date syrup, rose water, and roasted pine nuts)**
- **White of one egg**

**METHOD:** Shake all ingredients, strain, and serve over ice in a rocks glass.

**SERVING SUGGESTION:** Garnish with pan masala.

*Tu vas sortir ce soir?*

ARE YOU GOING OUT TONIGHT?

## Danico

**6 Rue Vivienne, 75002 Paris, France**
**+33 1 42 21 93 71**
**Price** ***
**Atmosphere: Chic and trendy Parisian**
**daroco.fr/**

Danico is a cocktail bar hidden within the trendy Italian eatery Darocco and brought to you by one of the cocktail industry's most highly regarded pros, Nico de Soto. You can access the bar either via the busy restaurant or come in the side door via the gorgeous Gallerie Vivienne. Bar and restaurant are located in what was once Jean Paul Gaultier's flagship store. The style is super chic with statement wallpaper, a cool graphic bar logo, and a sweet little seating area on the mezzanine. This is where on-trend adults with taste go for cocktails executed by impeccable bar staff in nautical shirts. Classics are always an option, but it's worth getting adventurous and trying some of the drinks made with more unusual ingredients like Pandan syrup or asparagus eau de vie.

## Dirty Dick

**10 Rue Frochot 75009 Paris**
**Price:** **
**Atmosphere: Tiki Time**

Situated in the trendy SoPi district, Dirty Dick is THE destination for top notch tropical and rum drinks in Paris. The usual decorative touches like masks and beachy murals plus two custom carved enormous totem poles transport you to an island state of mind. And, tiki cocktails are served in bespoke ceramic mugs from a local designer. A tropical bird soundtrack loops in the loos. This is where you go to let your hair down, and forget about the real world as you sip a perfectly made Mai Tai. Super friendly bar staff and a young and lively Parisian crowd notch up the party vibe. It's a must for tiki and rum lovers.

# — DE LA BRETAGNE —

Invented at the new CopperBay bar, this cocktail that celebrates Brittany is supposed to be served at room temperature.

- **1 oz. rye whiskey**
- **¾ oz. Pommeau de Bretagne**
- **½ oz. Bénédictine liqueur**
- **½ tablespoon hydromel like Tupelo Mead**
- **4 dashes anise extract (found in the baker's section at your grocer)**

**METHOD:** Pour all ingredients into a mixing glass without ice.

Aerate the liquid with a mini whisk and swizzle method.

**SERVING SUGGESTION:** Pour into tall hurricane glass rimmed with Cajun spices to create an emulsion.

> Pommeau de Bretagne is a light alcoholic drink made with apple juice and Calvados (apple brandy). You can find it at quality liquor stores.

## Experimental Cocktail Club (ECC)

**37 Rue Saint-Sauveur, 75002 Paris**
**Phone: 01 45 08 88 09**
**Price:** **
**Atmosphere: Speakeasy**
**experimentalcocktailclub.fr/**

This was the bar that changed everything in Paris and where the ECC group got its start. Going in now, it might not feel as groundbreaking as it was but back in 2007 when there were just hotel bars and bad bars (with a few exceptions). This groundbreaking lounge still looks and feels like a speakeasy: the small sign is hard to see, the ambiance is dark and sexy, and the drinks are heavenly. People took notice back then and a very cool crowd continues to make this intimate room their drinking hole.

"ECC started a new ice culture in Paris; we brought in the first American-style ice machines, which enabled us to offer a proper cocktail using all different types of ice."

+++

**Romée de Gorianinoff, one of the founders of ECC**

# — EXPÉRIENCE 1 —

One of the first cocktails created by Romée and his partners when they opened Experimental Cocktail Club. It's one of the first and only to survive the later cocktail lists at their various clubs around the world.

---

- **1¾ oz. vodka**
- **½ teaspoon fresh lemon juice**
- **½ teaspoon elderflower cordial**
- **2 fresh basil leaves**

---

**METHOD:** Shake the ingredients together with ice in your cocktail shaker. Strain twice and serve in a chilled martini glass.

**SERVING SUGGESTION:** ECC garnishes this drink with a lemon grass straw.

*Ça te dit d'aller boire un verre ?*

DO YOU WANT TO GET A DRINK?

## Fifty Fifty

**74 Rue Jean-Pierre Timbaud, 75011 Paris**
**+33 7 57 84 96 62**
**Price: ****
**Atmosphere: Youthful and fun**
**fifty-fifty-cocktail-bar.business.site/**

The bustling Oberkampf area is packed with bars offering happy hour pints and colorful shots. But if you know where to look, you can find the hidden gems where cocktail quality shines through. Fifty Fifty is a tiny bar that takes the fun neighborhood vibe and combines it with craft beer and beautifully presented craft cocktails. Owner, Hugo Gent's, passion for his project means a topnotch selection of ingredients, good range of spirits and interesting beer selection - including Corsican brands (where he's originally from.) It's a great example of the new generation of bars that are cool and laid back but still take their cocktails seriously.

## Fréquence

**20 Rue Keller, 75011 Paris**
**+ 33 1 71 32 40 35**
**Price: ****
**Ambience: Old school cool**
**facebook.com/frequenceparis/**

Fréquence has only been open a few years but is already making waves on the Paris cocktail scene and hitting internationally recognized lists like the World's 50 Best Discovery (always a good indication of what is up and coming in any city.) In addition to a seasonally changing cocktail menu, customers come here for the tunes. There is always something groovy coming from the record player thanks to their large selection of vinyl including reggae, soul and disco. DJ's regularly come to liven up nights that can go as late as 4am on weekends.

# — OLD CUBAN —

This is ECC's take on the cocktail originally created by Audrey Saunders of the Pegu Club.

- **Fresh mint leaves**
- **½ oz. fresh lime juice**
- **1⅓ oz. Ron Cubain Havana club 3 years (or your favorite premium white rum)**
- **½ oz. simple syrup**
- **1 barspoon of ginger cordial**
- **Billecart Salmon Brut Champagne to top**
- **2 dashes Angostura bitters on top**

**METHOD:** Shake all ingredients except the Champagne and bitters.

**SERVING SUGGESTION:** Serve in a chilled martini glass without ice. Top off with the Champagne and bitters.

## Jefrey's

**14 Rue Saint-Sauveur, 75002 Paris**
**Phone: 01 42 33 60 77**
**Price: ****
**Atmosphere: Intimate lounge**
**jefreys.fr/**

Sébastien Foulard manages this pocket-sized place modeled after an English gentleman's club. But this cocktail lounge is definitely not boys-only. Brice Martaud and Guillaume Hélin put their skills to work behind the bar to create concoctions that are difficult to replicate at home (although we encourage you to try with the Steve Casino on page 204) They are equally at home with classics as with cutting edge cocktails. If it's too busy downstairs, grab a comfortable spot in the small upstairs nook.

## Glass

**7 Rue Frochot, 75009 Paris, France**
**Phone: 09 80 72 98 83**
**Price: ****
**Atmosphere: Intimate**
**glassparis.com/**

In the now über-trendy So-Pi neighborhood is yet another late-night hotspot brought to you by the folks behind Candelaria. Try the John Doe, which contains Pisco flavored with dill, Fenet Branca, and their house-made lime cordial. It's light green, fresh, and delectable.

JEFREY'S

# — STEVE CASINO —

This recipe comes by way of the bar team at Jefry's. Noix de la St Jean is a French wine-based aperitif.

- **1 egg white**
- **1 3/4 oz. Peanut Oil-Infused Bourbon**
- **3/4 oz. Tonka syrup**
- **1/3 oz. Noix de la St Jean**
- **3/4 oz. fresh lemon juice**

**METHOD:** Add eggwhite to the shaker and shake vigorously for several seconds. Add remaining ingredients to the shaker and shake again. Pour into a rocks or old fashioned glass. Garnish with a peanut in its shell

For the Peanut Oil-Infused Bourbon, add several drops of peanut oil to bourbon. Let stand for a couple of days. Put in the freezer and remove the oil which will harden and float to the top.

# — BOBO PARISIEN —

This delightful cocktail comes from the ingenious brain of Guillaume at Jefrey's bar in the 2nd arrondissement, Paris.

- **1¾ oz. gin (Tanqueray preferred)**
- **½ oz. St-Germain**
- **½ oz. King L'Avion d'Or**
- **1 dash of rhubarb bitters**
- **The whites of one egg**
- **And a splash of club soda**

**METHOD:** Shake all ingredients together with ice in a cocktail shaker.

**SERVING SUGGESTION:** Serve in an oversized tea cup with a whole star anise floating in the froth and a sprinkling of Peychaud bitters. Watch your friends smile.

# — BLACK POINT À LA FRANÇAISE —

This is a strong drink for a whisky lover devised by Guillaume, the *chef du bar* at Jefrey's. It's important to serve it in a small, chilled sherry or port glass.

- **1½ oz. JW Double Black Whisky**
- **½ tablespoon Picon Club**
- **½ tablespoon Yellow Chartreuse**
- **1 teaspoon Grand Marnier**

**METHOD:** Mix all ingredients together and serve in an elegant Nick and Nora–style glass (sherry or port) and garnish with a dried orange round.

*Je prends, (un verre de rosé), s'il vous plaît.*

(FILL IN THE COCKTAIL NAME)

I'LL TAKE (A GLASS OF ROSE) PLEASE.

## Le Calbar

**82 Rue de Charenton, 75012 Paris**
**Phone: 01 84 06 18 90**
**Price: ****
**Atmosphere: A single girl's dream**
**lecalbarcocktail.com/**

Pretty quickly upon entering this bar you'll realize that the name is a play on the French words for boxers (Calecon) + bar because that's all the guys are wearing apart from their shirts. If you can take your eyes off of their legs, you'll enjoy the cool decor, black walls and all kinds of small paintings, small copper pots, and other bric-a-brac adorning *les murs.* Oh yeah, and the drinks are pretty darn good, too.

"Here our most popular drink is the 'Surprise Me,' which is when our bartenders make a bespoke cocktail just for you and the mood you are in."

+++

**Christophe Sichanh, bartender and co-founder at Calbar**

# — ROMEO À RIO —

A Brazilian Romeo is certainly fantasy worthy. Perhaps this will get you halfway there. By Romain Krot.

- **½ oz. red fruit syrup**
- **½ oz. fresh lemon juice**
- **1¾ oz. Cachaça (a Brazilian-made sugar cane liquor)**
- **1 barspoon of Liqueur de Violette**
- **A few mint sprigs**
- **1 egg white**

**METHOD:** Make red fruit syrup by infusing simple syrup with raspberries and strawberries. Cool and strain before use.

Shake ingredients dry (that is, without ice) and then wet (with ice), and strain into a chilled martini glass.

**SERVING SUGGESTION:** Sprinkle drink with smoked paprika.

> Liqueur de Violette (also Crème de Violette) is actually made with real violets by a number of different companies in France and elsewhere such as Briottet and Giffard. It is widely available online and at high-end liquor stores.

# — THE SMOKY SPICY MARGARITA —

The guys in their underwear at Calbar in Paris concocted this number, and yes, it's delish!

---

- **1⅓ oz. Mezcal vida**
- **½ tablespoon Islay whisky**
- **1 oz. fresh lime juice**
- **$^{3}/_{5}$ oz. homemade red pepper syrup (create this by adding spicy red peppers to your simple syrup and let stand as long as possible)**
- **½ tablespoon Campari**
- **3 dashes Thai bitters**

---

**METHOD:** Shake all ingredients with ice, double strain, and serve in a chilled martini glass and garnish with a dried orange wheel. Feel free to drink in your boxer shorts!

*Je voudrais votre meilleur cocktail.*

I'D LIKE TO HAVE YOUR BEST COCKTAIL.

## Le Mary Celeste

**1 Rue Commines, 75003 Paris**
**Phone: 09 80 72 98 83**
**Price: ****
**Atmosphere: Nautical**
**lemaryceleste.com/**

A refreshingly unique little bar decorated in white with a few pops of color. The sphere shaped bar is inviting, as is the variety of small bites on offer including oysters, which most other bars don't offer.

COCKTAILS
12 EUROS
VERRE
SINGLE LADIES
SEL GOSSE
RAIN DOG
EL CURADO
CAVALCANTI

## Le Syndicat

**51 rue Faubourg St Denis, 75010 Paris**
**Phone: 06 66 63 57 60**
**Price:** **
**Atmosphere: Urban grunge**
**syndicatcocktailclub.com/**

Le Syndicat is a fun and friendly place that focuses on 100% French ingredients for classics and creations. The concept became so popular they now have a sister bar in the 20th arrondissement of Paris called La Commune that focuses on serving delicious punch bowls. Plus the hip-hop soundtrack at le Syndicat creates a trés cool ambiance.

## Little Red Door

**60 rue Charlot, 75003 Paris**
**Phone: 09 83 58 93 32**
**Price: ******
**Atmosphere: Cocktail tavern**
**lrdparis.com/**

Don't attempt to actually enter the little red door like I did; instead open the actual door on the left and you won't feel so foolish. Have a seat at the bar and order up a Poor Willy's Mule or an Iggy. They are sincere about their craft at Little Red Door; interestingly, they add a douse of homemade saltwater to each recipe, which they feel brings all the ingredients together. And why not; chefs have been doing this forever in the kitchen. Located on the rue Charlot, one of the coolest streets in Paris, this hotspot sizzles with class and cocktail expertise.

# — IGGY —

This pop-star cocktail was invented at the Little Red Door in Paris.

---

- **1½ oz. Dolin Dry Vermouth**
- **¾ oz. Merlet Brothers Blend Cognac**
- **1 tablespoon Eucalyptus syrup**
- **4 dashes Braulio Italian bitter liqueur (or any Italian Amaro)**
- **Dash of salt solution**

---

**METHOD:** All of the ingredients are stirred over ice and then strained and served in a chilled martini glass.

**SERVING SUGGESTION:** Garnish with grapefruit zest.

## Lulu White

**12 Rue Frochot, 75009 Paris**
**Phone: 09 83 58 93 32**
**Price: ****
**Atmosphere: Paris meets New Orleans**
**luluwhite.bar/**

This absinthe bar named in honor of a renowned New Orleans Madame attempts to combine the spirit of Pigalle where it's located with sense of *Nouvelle Orleans*. The result is a charming and warm mélange with two Brits mixing drinks behind the bar. Even if you don't speak French you can learn a lot here about the new Paris cocktail culture by talking to Matthew Long, the head bartender. Absinthe is revered at Lulu White but fear not, they are expert at putting just a hint of it in their craftily made drinks.

# — MOONFLOWER —

Invented by Matthew Long, former head bartender at Lulu White, this is a push-me pull-you type of drink. Come down with the scotch and stay up with the coffee. Perfect when you need that pick-me-up at 11 p.m.

- **1½ oz. Chivas 12 Year Scotch**
- **2 oz. cold brew coffee (weaker coffee is best)**
- **½ oz. Dubonnet Rouge**
- **5 drops St. George Vert Absinthe**
- **1 tablespoon Perrier**

**METHOD:** Combine ingredients, except Perrier, in a mixing glass.

Gently stir for 3 seconds, strain into ice filled Collins glass, and add Perrier. Mix thoroughly.

**SERVING SUGGESTION:** Garnish with a lemon slice and a straw.

"LET ME BE MAD, THEN, BY ALL MEANS! MAD WITH THE MADNESS OF ABSINTHE, THE WILDEST, MOST LUXURIOUS MADNESS IN THE WORLD! VIVE LA FOLIE! VIVE L'AMOUR! VIVE L'ANIMALISME! VIVE LE DIABLE!"

*Marie Corelli, Wormwood: A Drama of Paris*

## Maria Loca

**31 Boulevard Henri IV, 75004 Paris**
**Phone: 01 42 77 51 95**
**Price: ****
**Atmosphere: Shipwrecked**
**marialoca.com/**

Head to Maria Loca if you like rum or cachaça; owner Michael and his partner are dead serious about the stuff. They take high-quality rum and add their own mix of spices to them or macerate walnuts in cachaça, adding to and playing with the liquors and then creating wholly unique cocktails with their new products. Try the Façon Maria or Le Woody Wood and you'll walk away for a whole new appreciation for these liquors. Close your eyes, listen to the reggae, take a sip or two, and you'll feel like you are at a beach bar in St. Bart's.

## Prescription Cocktail Club

**23 rue Mazarine, 75006 Paris**
**Phone: 09 50 35 72 87**
**Price: ****
**Atmosphere: Rendez-vous**
**prescriptioncocktailclub.com/**

This is the ECC outlet in Saint-Germain-des-Prés. with a larger space but the same successful formula: good service, superior bar craft, and dark and sexy ambiance. Order the Mazarinette, named in honor of the street that Prescription sits on, if you want something fruity and easy to drink.

# — MAZARINETTE —

This is the signature cocktail made at the Prescription Cocktail Club in the 6th, Saint-Germain-des-Prés.

- **1 tablespoon fresh lemon juice**
- **1 tablespoon homemade rhubarb juice**
- **1 oz. Gordon sloe gin liqueur (or your favorite sloe gin)**
- **¾ oz. gin**
- **1 oz. Sipsmith Summer Cup apéritif**
- **Champagne to top**

**METHOD:** Make your own rhubarb juice using frozen or fresh rhubarb, one bunch chopped into ¾-inch pieces. Cover with water and simmer for about 30 minutes. Strain through a mesh, cool, and your juice is ready to use. Can be stored in your refrigerator for up to a week.

Shake all items except Champagne with ice, strain into chilled martini glass, and serve neat, topped with Champagne.

**SERVING SUGGESTION:** Garnish with a strawberry.

Sipsmith is a small batch liquor company headquartered in the UK and partly owned by Jared Brown, one of the world's most well-known cocktail historians; coincidentally, I consulted him for this book. Their Summer Cup is a gin infused with the flavors of Earl Grey tea and lemon verbena grown by Jared himself, a very English gin indeed.

What's the difference between gin and sloe gin? Gin is a liquor traditionally made with juniper berries. Sloe gin is actually a liqueur, not a liquor, made with berries from the blackthorn bush and is red in color and sweet in taste.

## Red House

**1 bis Rue de la Forge Royale, 75011 Paris, France**
**Phone: 01 43 67 06 43**
**Price: ****
**Atmosphere: Manly grunge**

Late nights, a little grunge, an old school arcade game, real rock and roll on the radio—this is the kind of combo I can really get into. Red House feels very Brooklyn, yet you are right in the11th arrondissement, the *vrai* night life area of Paris. This is the perfect place to end up after a long night. Their Red House Old Fashioneds are delicious, and yeah, it's okay to get a little sloppy here.

## Rehab

**7 Rue de l'Échelle, 75001 Paris**
**Price: *****
**Atmosphere: Belle Epoque Shabby Chic**

Rehab combines two current cocktail trends in one beautiful bar with CBD cocktails served in a speakeasy hidden in the under-construction Hotel Normandy. This is not an easy bar to find, so you'll need to ask someone in the hotel reception area to "Please take me to Rehab" (S'il vous plaît, emmenez-moi à Rehab). You'll be transported to the Belle-Epoque era in this shabby chic boudoir inspired bar. It's a perfect spot for a fun girls night or a romantic evening a deux, maybe seated in the more intimate "opium bed."

# — RED HOUSE OLD FASHIONED —

Nobody makes an Old Fashioned like the Red House. Delicious!

- **1 cardamom seed**
- **1 oz. Jim Beam Rye**
- **½ oz. Bitter Truth Pimento Dram**
- **½ oz. Drambuie**

**METHOD:** Crush the cardamom in a mixing glass.

Add the remaining ingredients and stir with ice.

**SERVING SUGGESTION:** Serve on an ice ball (or large cube) in a double old-fashioned glass, garnished with a lemon peel and orange.

*Tout arrive en France!*

EVERYTHING HAPPENS IN FRANCE!
(FROM MAXIMES, RÉFLEXIONS MORALES BY
FRANÇOIS DE LA ROCHEFOUCAULD)

# — LIBERTINE —

A libertine is described as a free-thinker, a man who disregards the social norms, especially in regards to sexuality. Whoa, look out ladies! This comes courtesy of Jen Riley from Red House, Paris.

- **1 oz. vodka**
- **2 teaspoons Campari**
- **2 teaspoons simple syrup**
- **2 teaspoons fresh lemon juice**
- **1 tablespoon grapefruit juice**
- **½ oz. egg white**
- **1 barspoon rhubarb and ginger jam**

**METHOD:** Shake all ingredients together with ice in a shaker.

Double strain and shake again without ice to emulsify the egg white, then pour into a Champagne flute and top with ½ oz. Ruby Port.

"IN PARIS, IT WAS DIFFICULT FOR WOMEN AT BARS WHEN I FIRST STARTED. SOME PEOPLE WOULD HARDLY ORDER A DRINK FROM YOU BECAUSE THEY FELT LIKE YOU WOULDN'T KNOW WHAT YOU WERE DOING. FINALLY NOW I FEEL PARIS IS ON THE CUSP OF CHANGING WITH SO MANY MORE WOMEN BEHIND THE BAR; MEN ARE REALIZING WHAT A GREAT JOB WE'RE DOING."

+++

**JEN RILEY,**
**BARTENDER AT**
**RED HOUSE**

# — NIGHT BIRD —

A craft scotch cocktail by Jen Riley at Red House, Paris.

- **1¾ oz. Talisker Storm**
- **1 barspoon Calvados gum syrup**
- **5 dashes Creme de Violette**
- **2 drops Teapot Bitters (available online from Boker's Bitters)**

**METHOD:** Stirred over ice in a mixing glass and served into a chilled martini glass.

**SERVING SUGGESTION:** Garnish with a spray of bergamot essence.

> Bourbon isn't easily found in France, but if you prefer something a bit sweet, substitute bourbon in one of our whiskey recipes.

## — AUDEMUS CENTURY —

Created by Joseph Boley at Red House, Paris, one of the most rock and roll bars in Paris. Great for a late-night tipple.

---

- **1 oz. Pink Pepper Gin (made by Audemus)**
- **¾ oz. Cocchi Americano (similar to Dubonnet)**
- **¾ oz. Crème de Cacao Blanc (white chocolate liqueur)**
- **¾ oz. fresh lemon juice**

---

**METHOD:** Shake with ice in your shaker, strain, and pour into a chilled coupe glass neat.

**SERVING SUGGESTION:** Garnish with a lemon twist.

> At this time Audemus is only available in Europe and the UK. Until it is distributed in the U.S. and Canada you can make your own by adding ½ tablespoon of pink peppercorns to a bottle of gin and let it sit for at least a day but as long as possible. Audemus doesn't crack their peppercorns, but other DIY-ers do.

AUDEMUS
SPIRITS
CRÉATEUR DE SPIRITUEUX
PINK
PEPPER
GIN
500 ML
44% VOL

## Shake N' Smash

**87, rue de Turbigo, 75003 Paris**
**Phone: 01 42 72 30 76**
**Price: ****
**Atmosphere: Funky finesse**
**shakensmash.com/**

Jerome, the owner, is the fourth generation in business in the spot where his Corsican grandfather started a brasserie in 1923. Jerome recently changed the concept and created a true cocktail bar with a boudoir-style ambiance. Upon entry you might think you've entered a house of ill repute, but fear not; the only thing for sale is dangerously delicious cocktails and French-style tapas. I was wowed by the presentation and the taste of l'Education Sentimentale. It's inspired by the Flaubert novel and served on a page of the book in a Cognac glass laying on its side on crushed ice with caramelized apples sticking out of the ice. The interior decor maybe funky, but Jerome is dead serious about his creative concoctions.

## Sherry Butt

**20, rue Beautreillis Paris 75004**
**Price: *****
**Atmosphere: Cool, modern day French whisky bar**
**sherrybuttparis.com**

Sherry Butt's name is taken from the xérès casks in which whisky is sometimes aged and gives a clue as to what you'll find inside this trendy bar: a huge selection of whiskies from around the world. You can 'travel' through whisky flights or just enjoy one of their excellent cocktails. The team behind this bar has some serious cocktail cred, so the drinks will never disappoint. The space is stylish with comfortable sofas, wood floors and stone walls all with distressed details that make it casually chic. The ceiling window lets in nice light to illuminate those gorgeous cocktails.

## Sister Midnight

**4 rue Viollet-le-Duc 75009 Paris**
**+33 6 74 39 32 20**
**Ambience: Uber cool with an edge**
**sistermidnightparis.com/**

Joseph Boley and Jen Riley of Red House have added another hotspot to the popular nightlife area of Pigalle with their latest project, Sister Midnight. This bar boldly mixes grit and glam with a rock 'n' roll attitude and on-point cocktails. You can get a steller classic here or go for one of their house creations, like the spicy Suicide, which is completely out of the ordinary. If you're feeling peckish they also have cheese platters with pickles from the cool-as-heck local catering duo, Emperor Norton. Plus they have a regular calendar of drag burlesque nights.

## Solera Paris

**283 Rue Saint-Jacques, 75005 Paris**
**+ 33 7 77 60 63 93**
**Price: *****
**Atmosphere: Left bank cocktail lounge**
**soleraparis.wixsite.com/solera/qui-sommes-nous**

This left bank cocktail lounge is run by Christopher Gaglione who formerly worked at high end hotel bars and brings that level of service to a more accessible cocktail experience. What he also brings is some standout creative cocktail staging. Expect drinks served in a smoking genie lamp, beautiful porthole vessels or under bell jars. Gaglione has created a concept of a "fooddrinks" experience and focuses on pairing cocktails and small plates for a full gustatory package.

## The Cambridge Public House

**8 Rue de Poitou, 75003 Paris**
**Price: ****
**Atmosphere: Franco-Anglo gastro pub**
**thecambridge.paris/**

The Cambridge Public House mixes craft cocktails with tasty British pub snacks for a fun Anglo-Franco food and drink mash-up. The cocktail menu changes seasonally with a focus on fresh ingredients and includes a good selection of mocktails as well. The team behind the bar work with local partners, so bread, coffee, and wines come from quality fellow French businesses. And, in a city with limited options when it comes to day drinks, it's nice to know of a venue that opens from 3:00 p.m., seven days a week.

# — FUEGO DE COLIMA —

This inventive cocktail that combines ginger and lemongrass to tickle your taste buds is by Jerome at Shake N' Smash.

- **1¾ oz. Calle 23 tequila (any other good tequila)**
- **¾ oz. ginger and lemongrass cordial (see recipe below)**
- **2 teaspoons Chairman's Reserve Spiced Rum**
- **1 tablespoon sugar syrup**

**FIRST, THE GINGER AND LEMONGRASS CORDIAL:** A ginger and lemongrass non-alcoholic cordial is made by Bottlegreen in Britain but tough to source in the States. So here's how you can make your own. You'll need: a large nob of ginger peeled and sliced, and a stick of lemongrass (crush the white part and chop finely discarding any green parts). Add ginger and lemongrass to 2 cups water and 1½ cups sugar. Let sugar dissolve over the heat on simmer as you would any simple syrup. Let the flavors simmer together for about 20 minutes. Cool, strain, and add to a jar storing it in the fridge up to two weeks or more.

**METHOD:** Mix all ingredients together and shake with ice.

**SERVING SUGGESTION:** Served in a chilled coupe glass.

# — ESQUISSE №. 1 —

An esquisse is a preliminary sketch. This sketch was created by Jerome at Shake N' Smash, Paris.

- **1¾ oz. Grey Goose Pear (or other pear vodka)**
- **1½ oz. white chardonnay grape juice by Alain Millat (or other fine-quality white grape juice)**
- **4 teaspoons fresh squeezed grapefruit**
- **4 teaspoons fresh lime**
- **1½ tablespoon homemade vanilla syrup (or substitute other vanilla syrup, like Monin, for example)**

**METHOD:** Place all ingredients in a cocktail shaker with ice and shake vigorously.

Strain and serve in a coupe glass.

**SERVING SUGGESTION:** Hang several grapes over the edge of the glass, as well as a slice of fresh pear that's been soaked in lemon juice and water so that it doesn't brown.

"IT'S ALL ABOUT THE ART AND PASSION OF THE CREATION AND THE INGREDIENTS."

+++

**JEROME, OWNER OF SHAKE N' SMASH**

# — BURLESQUE —

This recipe comes from the cool craft beer and cocktail bar Fifty Fifty:

- **1 fresh cucumber round**
- **1⅔ oz. Beefeater Gin**
- **⅓ oz. Chambord**
- **⅔ oz. fresh lemon juice**
- **¼ oz. simple syrup**
- **4 drops Burlesque Bittermens Bitter**

**METHOD:** Muddle the cucumber in a shaker until it is completely broken down. Add other ingredients and fill the shaker ⅔ full with ice. Shake well and double strain into a chilled coupette. Garnish with a cucumber ribbon woven onto a wooden pick.

# Unique

This group of bars in Paris were founded on a theme or an area of interest that the owners are passionate about. These will be difficult to find elsewhere, and if they spur your imagination as they did mine, go ahead and belly up to the bar.

## Comptoir Generale

**80 quai de Jemmapes, Paris 75010**
**Phone: 01 44 88 24 48**
**Price: ***
**Atmosphere: Eclectic & blooming**
**lecomptoirgeneral.com/**

Places like this in Paris are priceless. Creativity rules here; it's a gallery, it's a museum, a bookshop, a café, and yeah, there are cocktails. Their signature cocktail is Secousse with bissap, a Senegalese liqueur made from hibiscus flowers. I love the high ceilings, the quirky flea market décor, and the general vibe. They call it a museum of ghetto culture; I call it wonderful.

## Gossima Ping Pong Bar

**4 Rue Victor Gelez, 75011 Paris**
**Phone: 09 67 29 75 79**
**Price: ****
**Atmosphere: Competitive fun**
**gossima.fr/**

The Gossima Ping Pong bar is the place to go with a bunch of friends. It's ideal for students and anyone who enjoys ping pong, but it's also hip and serves up a mean cocktail. Talk to Thomas at the bar; he'll invent something for you. Or, sample his Conquistador, which is kind of like a margarita but made with a touch of chocolate, cacao, and spice.

# — LA CONQUISTADOR —

Created by Nicolas and the boys at the super fun Ping Pong bar.

- **½ oz. Téquila Olmeca Reposado**
- **½ oz. Téquila Olmeca Silver**
- **1 tablespoon de liqueur de cacao blanc by Giffard**
- **½ oz. fresh lime juice**
- **1 teaspoon agave syrup**
- **5–7 dashes Aztec chocolate bitters by Fee Bros.**

**METHOD:** Combine all ingredients in a cocktail shaker with ice, shake, and strain.

**SERVING SUGGESTION:** Serve in a rocks glass with spicy salt on the rim and a lime wedge.

*Il est très mignon, le barman!*

THE BARTENDER IS REALLY CUTE!

# — LE PULPEUX —

Created by Nicolas Servettaz at the Gossima Ping Pong Bar, this is a refreshing cocktail for summer.

- **1½ oz. Beefeater Gin**
- **½ oz. thyme liqueur (Bigallet brand)**
- **½ oz. grapefruit juice**
- **½ oz. fresh lime juice**

**METHOD:** Mix all ingredients in a cocktail shaker with ice, strain, and serve over ice in a highball glass with ice and top with ginger beer.

**SERVING SUGGESTION:** Serve with a cucumber round and perhaps a fresh thyme sprig.

*Que la fête commence!*

LET THE PARTY BEGIN!

## Wall St. Bar

**17 Avenue Parmentier, 75011 Paris**
**Phone: 06 62 12 15 91**
**Price: ***
**Atmosphere: New York Stock Exchange**
**wallstreetbar.fr/**

If you ever dreamed of drinking at the Stock Exchange, you've come to the right place. What is lacking in ambiance is made up by the inventive concept of paying for your drinks depending on the fluctuations of the ticker. Your martini may go up or down as the clock ticks on, and it pays to order quickly when you see the price drop. Several times a night there's a stock market crash and drinks go down to their base levels; then you must shout out your order in the hundred seconds that remain.

# — COFFEE OLD FASHIONED —

This delicious drink was created by Candace Knyf as Death by Burrito's special during Paris' first-ever cocktail week in January 2015.

- **2 oz. tequila reposado infused with coffee**
- **1 barspoon agave syrup**
- **3 dashes Angostura bitters**

**METHOD:** First, infuse the tequila reposado with coffee. Put 3 barspoons of coffee in a filter submerged in 6 oz. of the tequila and let sit 4 hours to soak in the flavor. Light a stick of cinnamon until it smolders on one end. Place on a plate and cover it with a rocks glass so the smoke accumulates in the glass. Combine the remaining ingredients in a mixing glass. Upend the rock glass and strain the drink into it adding a few cubes of ice.

# — FAÇON MARIA —

Created by the charming Michael Landart at Maria Loca bar on Blvd Henri IV in Paris.

- 1¾ oz. Maria Loca Spiced Rum (or Chairman's Reserve Spiced Rum)
- 3 dashes Angostura bitters
- 1 barspoon Virgin Cane Honey

**METHOD:** Stir rum, bitters, and honey together in a cocktail glass with ice, and strain.

**SERVING SUGGESTION:** Serve over ice in an old-fashioned glass, no garnish.

"MARIA LOCA IS NAMED AFTER THE ILLEGAL ALCOHOL THAT THEY MAKE IN PRISON FROM WHATEVER SCRAPS THEY CAN GET. WHERE THERE'S A WILL..."

+++

**MICHAEL LANDARF,**
**CO-OWNER OF MARIA LOCA**

# — LE WOODY WOOD —

A creative cocktail by a creative man, Michael Landart, co-founder of Maria Loca.

- **1⅓ oz. Cachaça infused with walnuts (the liquor only needs 30–60 minutes to infuse)**
- **½ oz. Calvados**
- **1 tablespoon Bénédictine**
- **1 tablespoon Orange Curacao**

**METHOD:** Serve ingredients on ice in a large wine glass and strain.

**SERVING SUGGESTION:** Hang half a walnut over the edge of the glass, and serve with a cinnamon stick swizzle.

*Faire un tabac*

BEING THE TOAST OF THE TOWN

# London

## Coupette

**423 Bethnal Green Road London, United Kingdom E2 0AN.**
**+44 20 7729 9562**
**Price: ****
**Atmosphere: Modern day French cocktail lounge**
**coupette.co.uk/Coupette**

Coupette is "inspired by France, but proudly London" and a beautiful example of a French touch applied to food and drink abroad. In the handful of years it has been open, the bar has won awards for its quality cocktails, which are delicious to drink and lovely to look at. The team works with Calvados producers to serve various expressions of this famous French apple brandy as well as use it in tasty canned cocktails. Francophile or not, this is a worthwhile stop while in London. And don't miss their top notch cheese and charcuterie board!

## Experimental Cocktail Club

**13 a Gerrard St., Chinatown, London W1D 5PS**
**+44 20 7434 3559**
**Price: ****
**Atmosphere: Chinatown speakeasy**
**chinatownecc.com/**

Naturally, London is important enough to score its own ECC brought to you by the boys from Paris. This version stays with the speakeasy theme, so you'll have to hunt it down in London's Chinatown. Once inside you'll find the same boudoir charm and strong, spirited cocktails.

# Montreal

## Le Lab

**1351 Rachel East Montreal H2J 2K2, Canada**
**(514) 544-1333**
**Price:** **
**Atmosphere: Mad scientist**
**barlelab.com/**

Let's face it—everything has a French spin in Montreal; it's the French-est city we've got in North America even though most of its residents also speak perfect English. Enter Le Lab, where cocktail culture is turned upside down. Cocktails with beef jerky in them, cocktails on fire, bartenders who juggle—no, this is not a literal circus bar; it's a cocktail lab where almost anything goes.

# Toronto

## La Société (LS)

**131 Bloor St. W. #211 Toronto, ON M5S 1R1, Canada**
**(416) 551-9929**
**Price:** **
**Atmosphere: Classic tavern**
**toronto.lasociete.ca/**

With a long zinc bar and a stained glass ceiling that is reminiscent of La Coupole or Bofinger in Paris, La Société will make any Francophile feel at home. Sit at the bar, share a petit seafood tower, and savor your French cocktails, such as Confort Parisien or the French Derby. You won't feel far from France.

# Vancouver

## Tableau Bar & Bistro

**1181 Melville St. Vancouver, BC V6E 0A3, Canada**
**(604) 639-8692**
**Price:** **
**Atmosphere: Posh bistro**
**tableaubarbistro.com/**

Try a De la Louisianne cocktail made with rye, sweet vermouth, Bénédictine, bitters, and absinthe, or a Delmonico mixed with Hennessy, sweet and dry vermouth, gin, and bitters. Share some moules frites with a friend in Tableau's beautifully stylish room.

"London is a riddle. Paris is an explanation."

*G.K. Chesterton*

## — UMAMI MARTINI —

Umami is an entirely new class of liquor. Made in the Cognac region of France by Audemus Spirits, the idea was to come up with a savory liquor to use in savory drinks. Umami uses cornichons as well as over twenty other secret spices to flavor this liquor like the fifth taste, umami. So far it's available in France and the UK. If you can get your hands on it, you've got to try the Umami Martini.

---

- **White vermouth for rinsing a frozen glass**
- **2 oz. Umami**

---

**METHOD:** Rinse a frozen martini glass with ice and white vermouth and discard both.

Pour 2 oz. Umami into the glass.

**SERVING SUGGESTION:** Serve with an olive or two!

"A MAN MUST DEFEND HIS HOME, HIS WIFE, HIS CHILDREN, AND HIS MARTINI."

—*Jackie Gleason*

AUDEMUS
SPIRITS
CRÉATEUR DE SPIRITUEUX
UMAMI
500 ML
42% VOL

# — BLOODY UMAMI —

And then you'll want to bring that fifth taste to the classic Bloody Mary.

- **1½ oz. umami**
- **¾ cup of tomato juice**
- **2 dashes of Worstershire sauce**
- **1 dash (or more as desired) or Tabasco**
- **1 dash of celery bitter**
- **Salt and pepper to taste**

**METHOD:** Create this drink in your rocks glass with ice starting with the flavorings and then adding the Umami and then the tomato juice.

**SERVING SUGGESTION:** Stir and garnish with a lemon peel, a celery stick, a pickled green been, several olives or all of the above.

*Allons-y pour prendre un apéro.*

LET'S GO FOR A DRINK (AN APERITIF).

# — FRANCOPHILE IN THE USA —

WHISKY SOUR CERISE 250

SAZERAC 254

VIEUX CARRÉ 255

PINK PANTHER 259

JOY DIVISION 261

SADE'S TABOO 262

BARON OF BROOKLYN 263

MAISON ABSINTHE COLADA 265

THE LAST WORD 275

Americans' love of France goes back hundreds of years and, contrary to what you may have heard, the French are quite keen on the U.S. as well. There is nary a Parisian who won't tell you how much they love New York City, California, and Miami. There are certain towns in the U.S. that have an ingrained Frenchness to their culture, namely New Orleans. And, the French revere this great town, too. Who doesn't love a place that invented jazz and the Sazerac? There are loads of French people living stateside and they need places to drink. Thanks to the Alliance Française and a number of other French organizations, there is an interest in France all over the States. With that Francophile passion, you'll find bars and bistros serving up un petite slice of Paris daily.

# — WHISKY SOUR CERISE —

A French-ified version of a true American classic.

- **1½ oz. Brenne Whisky (or another sweet whisky such as Jameson's)**
- **1–2 oz. fresh lemon juice**
- **1½ teaspoons simple syrup**
- **1½ teaspoons Luxardo maraschino liqueur**
- **Cherries for garnish**

**METHOD:** Add all ingredients in a cocktail shaker with ice. Shake, strain and serve over ice in a rocks glass.

**SERVING SUGGESTION:** Garnish with Luxardo maraschino cherries or other cocktail cherries.

# Classic Cocktails & French Cheese Pairing Party

Cocktail and cheese experts, Forest Collins of 52 Martinis and Jennifer Greco of Chez Loulou, are the pioneers when it comes to pairing cocktails and cheese. This Paris-based pair has been working on their Cocktails x Cheese project for years, researching combos and offering workshops. They happily shared their tips on hosting your own DIY cocktails and French cheese pairing session for an elegantly easy way to entertain at home:

Invite 4 or 5 of your favorite Francophile girlfriends--a number small enough to fit comfortably around your table is best.

Choose one classic cocktail that everyone in the group loves.

Shop for five to ten different French cheeses, getting a range from the different cheese families.

Set the table with napkins, small tasting plates, knives and forks. Optionally you can add bread, but we like to taste cheese on its own.

Find a fantastic French soundtrack for your background music. Go with the classic Piaf or shake it up with a bit of Étienne Daho for a throwback to an 80's synth groove.

Don't forget to put a big carafe of water and glasses out to stay hydrated!

Taste through the cheeses one at a time, taking a sip before and after each bite.

Work through your cheese from mildest to strongest in flavor.

Take notes and discuss how one affects the other in terms of flavor and mouthfeel. You can even print tasting note sheets with

the name of the cocktail at the top and a column or row for each cheese.

Find your perfect pairing and voila! You now have a foolproof method for an elegantly easy cocktail hour or perfect after-dinner drinks and cheese combo.

For an even easier way to elevate your entertainment, skip the DIY workshop and just invite your friends around for cocktail hour employing one or all three of these surefire pairings, recommended by Jennifer and Forest. Either serve the cocktails one at a time with a side of the cheese or put out a board with all three and offer the choice of cocktails. You're also not restricted to serving the cheese on its own and can melt it on toasted baguette slices or use the harder cheeses in gougeres. These combinations include French cheeses that are easier to source in the U.S..

# — SAZERAC —

Created at the Roosevelt Hotel in New Orleans, this is a classic American cocktail with French origins.

- **½ teaspoon absinthe, or Herbsaint (a New Orleans brand of anise liqueur)**
- **1 teaspoon simple syrup**
- **4 dashes Peychaud bitters**
- **1 small dash Angostura bitters**
- **2 oz. rye whiskey**
- **Strip of lemon peel**

**METHOD:** Fill a rocks glass with ice that has been coated with absinthe or Herbsaint. Blend the whiskey and bitters with the simple syrup in a cocktail glass with ice and stir. Strain this mixture into your rocks glass with the ice.

**SERVING SUGGESTION:** Rub lemon peel on the rim and serve with the peel on the rim and not in the drink.

> Originally a Sazerac was made with Cognac, absinthe, a sugar cube, and three dashes of Pechaud's bitters, which was made in New Orleans by a local apothecary. Later Rye was substituted for the Cognac when French vineyards fell to the Phylloxera epidemic in the 1860s. Herbsaint replaced absinthe when it was banned in the U.S. in 1912. The Sazerac remains by law New Orleans' official cocktail.

# — VIEUX CARRÉ —

Created in New Orleans in the 1930s this is as classic a Nawlins' cocktail as you can get. It is French for the *Old Square,* which refers to the French quarter.

- **¾ oz. rye whiskey**
- **¾ oz. Cognac**
- **¾ oz. sweet vermouth**
- **A dash of both Peychaud's and Angostura bitters**
- **½ teaspoon of Bénédictine liqueur**

**METHOD:** Shake all ingredients in your cocktail shaker with ice, strain, and serve in a Nick and Nora glass neat or in a rocks glass on the rocks. Garnish with a cherry.

Peychaud's bitters are made in Louisiana.

*Laissez les bons temps rouler!*

LET THE GOOD TIMES ROLL!

(NOTE: THIS IS STRICTLY AN EXPRESSION IN LOUISIANA, NOT FRANCE.)

## New Orleans, Louisiana

### The Sazerac Bar

**130 Roosevelt Way, The Roosevelt, New Orleans, LA 70112**
**Phone: (504) 648-1200**
**Price: ****
**Atmosphere: Uptown chic**
**therooseveltneworleans.com/dining/the-sazerac-bar.html**

Located in the Roosevelt hotel, this is *the* spot where the Sazerac was invented back in the 1850s. The potent combination of Herbsaint (a New World version of absinthe), Rye from America and Peychaud's bitters from New Orleans emerges as a melting pot of cultures in a glass. The bar remains stylish, uptown, and the picture-perfect place to try your first Sazerac.

### Bouligny Tavern

**3641 Magazine St., New Orleans, LA 70115**
**Phone: (504) 891-1810**
**Price: ****
**Atmosphere: Mod lounge**
**boulignytavern.com/**

Hipster and mid-century modern fanatics flock to this cocktail lounge on Magazine Street at all hours of the night. Try a White Melrose made with Basque cider while you tuck into their Gouda beignets, duck confit Brussels sprouts, or foie gras brioche. This is sipping and snacking in style!

### French 75

**813 Bienville St., New Orleans, LA 70112**
**Phone: (504) 523-5433**
**Price: ****
**Atmosphere: Classic through and through**
**arnaudsrestaurant.com/**

Located in Arnaud's, one of Nola's oldest restaurants, French 75 was named one of the best bars in America by *Esquire* magazine. Picture cozy club chairs, overhead fans, servers in white coats, and dark polished wood. This is your Grandpa's bar that serves a mean French 75. A classic cocktail in a classic cocktail bar that has never gone out of style.

## Jean Lafitte's Old Absinthe House 1807

**240 Bourbon St., New Orleans, LA 70112**
**Phone: (504) 523-3181**
**Price: ***
**Atmosphere: Heavy day drinking acceptable**
**ruebourbon.com/oldabsinthehouse/**

Oscar Wilde drank at this more-than-200-year-old watering hole in the French quarter of the most French city in America. Try the signature Absinthe House frappé in this casual pub adorned with football helmets. This is a place where locals and tourists happily meet to knock back a few. Drinking begins at 9 a.m.!

## Napoleon House

**500 Chartres St., New Orleans, LA 70130**
**Phone: (504) 524-9752**
**Price: ***
**Atmosphere: French Louisiana**
**napoleonhouse.com/**

Created for Napoleon back in 1821 as a refuge from his troubles in France. Napoleon never ended up here but you'll feel his spirit in this dark, funky, almost decrepit bar and café. The place oozes that casual Louisianan charm, and the combo of a muffuletta sandwich (a Nola classic) and a ginger mint Pimm's Cup cocktail makes for a refreshingly delicious afternoon.

# New York

There are more than 50,000 Frenchmen and women living in New York City, and most others that aren't French are huge Paris fans. So it's not surprising that in Manhattan and Brooklyn, you'll find a plethora of French-owned or -inspired places: stores, restaurants, bistros, crêperies, boulangeries, and yes, French cocktail bars.

# — PINK PANTHER —

DJ Max August of New York created this scrumptious number for my book. What a sweetie. Yes, I'm prejudiced; he's my son, but he was trained as a bartender.

---

- **2 oz. Grey Goose vodka**
- **1 oz. St-Germain (or any elderflower liqueur)**
- **Juice combo made from; ½ fresh grapefruit, ½ lime and ½ lemon**
- **Grottissimo cherry**

---

**METHOD:** Shake the above ingredients in a cocktail shaker with ice.

Strain and serve in a high-ball glass with ice, and top off with Lorina all-natural sparkling French lemonade.

**SERVING SUGGESTION:** Garnish with a Grottissimo cherry and a barspoon of the brandy that they come in to make it pink!

> Lorina all-natural sparkling French lemonade is available at fine gourmet grocers.

## — JOY DIVISION —

This cocktail comes courtesy of Phil Ward, bartender at Death & Co., New York City.

- 2 oz. Beefeater London dry gin
- 1 oz. Dolin dry vermouth
- ½ oz. triple sec or Cointreau
- 3 dashes absinthe (Vieux Pontarlier brand is preferred)
- 1 lemon twist

**METHOD:** Stir all the ingredients over ice, then strain into a coupe glass.

**SERVING SUGGESTION:** Garnish with a lemon twist.

"OUR NAME, DEATH & CO., IS DERIVED FROM A PLAQUE FROM THE PROHIBITION ERA THAT ILLUSTRATED THAT THE SLIDE DOWNHILL STARTS AT HANGING OUT AT THE SODA FOUNTAINS AND HOTEL BARS WHICH LEADS TO COCKTAILS, DRUGS, AND DEATH."

+++

**DAVID KAPLAN, FOUNDER OF DEATH & CO.**

# — SADE'S TABOO —

Jessica Gonzalez from Death & Co. authored this little number.

---

- **2 oz. high-quality Cognac (Hine is preferred)**
- **¾ oz. Cocchi Americano**
- **¾ oz. red vermouth (Dolin is preferred but any sweet vermouth may be substituted)**
- **1 dash Bittermans grapefruit bitters**

---

**METHOD:** Stir all the ingredients over ice, then strain into a coupe glass. No garnish needed.

# — BARON OF BROOKLYN —

Maison Premiere, a French bar in Williamsburg, is probably the most famous and difficult-to-get-into joint in this hipster enclave just across the water from Manhattan. It's only fitting, then, that they create a title such as this.

- **1 dash mole**
- **1 dash Angostura bitters**
- **½ oz. Suze**
- **½ oz. Crème du Banane**
- **1½ oz. Tawny Port**
- **1½ oz. Avua cachaça (or any other premium cachaça)**

**METHOD:** Mix everything in a cocktail class with ice, stir, strain, and serve in a brandy snifter with one large ice cube.

**SERVING SUGGESTION:** Garnish with a long lemon horse-neck twist.

Twists—there are several kinds. The one most of us know is the basic twist: use a pairing knife or a vegetable scraper and take some of the peel off a piece of citrus that is fairly wide and about 2 inches long max. You can then cut it down to be thinner if you wish. For a horse-neck, peel around the lemon (or other citrus) to create a spiral; these are about three times as long as a normal twist and are used when you want to start the twist down deep in the glass and or let it hang in and then over as opposed to floating on top.

## Maison Premiere

**298 Bedford Ave., Brooklyn, NY 11211**
**Phone: (347) 335-0446**
**Price:** **
**Atmosphere: Where the cool "kids" hang**
**maisonpremiere.com/**

This horseshoe-shaped bar and tiny restaurant takes its inspiration from Chez Janou in the Marais. The classic working absinthe fountain, thirty kinds of oysters, and the huge selection of absinthe on offer makes this gorgeous yet intimate bar a home-run for any of the cool kids who can squeeze their way in.

> TRICKS TO GETTING INTO MAISON PREMIERE: Open 7 days, 365 from 4 p.m. to 4 a.m. People line up at 3:30 p.m. to enjoy their $1 oyster happy hours. Don't do the same. Wait until the rush is over and head in at 5 or 5:30 p.m. on a Monday or Tuesday night, but be prepared to put your cell number down on the iPad and wait to land a stool in this always-packed hot-spot.

# — MAISON ABSINTHE COLADA —

A take on the classic piña colada with an absinthe twist via Maxwell Britten of Maison Premiere, Williamsburg, Brooklyn, New York.

- **1 oz. absinthe**
- **½ oz. Rhum JM (a type of rhum agricole)**
- **1 teaspoon Crème de Menthe**
- **1 oz. pineapple juice**
- **½ oz. lemon juice**
- **1 oz. coconut syrup**

**METHOD:** Combine ingredients and serve in a hurricane glass.

**SERVING SUGGESTION:** Maison Premiere serves this with a sprig of mint and a red-and-white paper straw. And for the absinthe, they use Mansinthe, the singer Marilyn Manson's own brand of absinthe made in Switzerland.

> Rhum agricole is made with fresh sugarcane juice. Industrial rum, which most of us buy, is made from molasses. For rum aficionados, rhum agricole, which has a stronger taste and flavor, is preferred and is considered an artisanal ingredient.

## Cherche-Midi

**282 Bowery, New York, NY 10012**
**Phone: (212) 226-3055**
**Price:** **
**Atmosphere: Perfect if you're dreaming of Paris**
**cherchemidiny.com/**

Sip a Wise Norman (a Calvados creation with sage) and munch on a crispy frogs leg and dream of Paris in Keith McNally's newest French-inspired bar/resto. After cocktails at the bar, why not stay awhile and sink into the kitchen's steak frites and a bottle of burgundy.

## Experimental Cocktail Club

**191 Chrystie St., New York, NY 10002**
**Price:** **
**Atmosphere: Vintage vogue**
**experimentalcocktailclubny.com/**

Romée De Goriainoff brought his team's unparalleled creativity to U.S. shores several years ago at their lower east side outpost of his famed Experimental Cocktail Club. Enjoy complex and creative concoctions created by the ECC team in the vintage-chic cocktail lounge and simply pretend you are in Paris.

## The Top of the Standard

**848 Washington St., New York, NY 10014**
**Phone: (212) 645-4646**
**Price:** ***
**Atmosphere: 40s and 50s glamour**
**standardhotels.com/high-line/food-drink/the-top-of-the-standard**

After reserving, head up to the Top of the Standard at the Standard Highline hotel for 1940s glamour and a kick-ass view of New York's skyline. It's a dressy adult-bar experience that you'd pull from your dreams of 1950s Paris and New York City.

*La vérité est dans le vin.*

IN WINE THERE IS TRUTH.

# Los Angeles

Los Angeles has its own style to be sure, but even tanned Hollywood hipster types want to retreat to the old world of France some nights.

## Bar Bouchon

**235 N Canon Drive, Beverly Hills, CA 90210**
**Phone: (310) 271-9910**
**Price: *****
**Atmosphere: Parisian chic**
**thomaskeller.com/**

Created by Thomas Keller of French laundry fame, this zinc bar simply reeks of Paris. Snack on truffle popcorn or the rilette of the day while sipping on a classic Moscow Mule served in the appropriate copper mug. The Provençal tile and the French waiters help transport you thousands of miles away from Beverly Hills and 90210.

## Little Door

**8164 W 3rd St., Los Angeles, CA 90048**
**Phone: (323) 951-1210**
**Price: ****
**Atmosphere: French countryside**
**thelittledoor.com/**

Whenever you ask an Angelino where to go to get your French on, they mention the Little Door. Try a Grandfather cocktail made with bourbon, calvados, and Italian vermouth, and sit outside after the main dining hours at either the new Santa Monica or their original location. Share a duck mousse pâté and enjoy the French country charm.

> Rilettes are similar to pâtés but much easier to make. Meat or fish is cubed or shredded, salted, cooked over low heat, then cured with the animal's own fat and stored in a crock. Served at room temperature and spread over toast. Made with pork, salmon, or another meat—if you see rillettes on a menu, order one as quickly as possible. Fatty deliciousness.

### Pour Vous

**5574 Melrose Ave., Los Angeles, CA 90038**
**Phone: (323) 871-8699**
**Price: ****
**Atmosphere: Sexy**
**pourvousla.com/**

This elegant Parisian cocktail lounge on Melrose in West Hollywood gives off a very sexy vibe. Whisper to your date that you'd like a *ménage à trois,* and he just might be fooled into thinking you didn't just order one of their French-inspired cocktails. The red banquets and fringed low-lit table lamps will get you in the mood.

## San Francisco

San Francisco has long been a town enamored with all things French. As of late, there has been a strong trend of French focused bars and brasseries. Heading up their drink menus are beaucoup de cocktails made with French absinthes, Cognacs, Chartreuse, and Calvados.

### Trou Normand

**140 New Montgomery St., San Francisco, CA 94105**
**Phone: (415) 975-0876**
**Price: ****
**Atmosphere: Northern French traditional**
**trounormandsf.com/**

This bar and restaurant was named for the northern French tradition of a small sip of brandy, often Calvados, drunk between courses to settle the stomach and reawaken the palate—a lovely, if dangerous idea. The bar itself is stunning, the huge sketch of a female nude behind the bar compelling, and the nose-to-tail whole butchery concept terribly French. Order a classic Corpse Reviver and nosh on house-made headcheese and pork pâté with fennel.

## Gaspar Brasserie

**185 Sutter St., San Francisco, CA 94104**
**(415) 576-8800**
**Price: ****
**Atmosphere: 1950s chic**
**gasparbrasserie.com/**

Try a quintessential French absinthe like Vieux Pontarlier in Gaspar's Absinthe frappe cocktail while sitting at the 1950s-inspired bar in San Fran's financial district. Stay longer to enjoy their briny oysters, magret de canard, and cassoulet beans. But whatever you do, don't order the Forget Paris cocktail; it may be tasty, but even in stunning San Francisco, Paris must never be forgotten.

## Monseiur Benjamain

**451 Gough St., San Francisco, CA 94102**
**(415) 402-2233**
**Price: ****
**Atmosphere: Opera stop**
**monsieurbenjamin.com/**

Try the Ace with whiskey and calvados, rosemary, and gin served in a Nick and Nora era glass while chomping on some camembert beignets. This slick modern bar and restaurant is the perfect stop before a night at the Symphony or the Opera house, both of which are walking distance away.

## Urchin Bistrot

**584 Valencia St., San Francisco, CA 94110**
**(415) 861-1844**
**Price: ****
**Atmosphere: Farmhouse bistro**
**urchinbistrot.com/**

Inspired by the Bistronomique movement in France, a husband-wife duo has opened this modern French bistro adding a fourth feather in their cap of culinary outposts. Belly up to the long wooden bar and order one of their artistically made, French-themed cocktails.

## Bar Agricole

**355 11th St., San Francisco, CA 94103**
**(415) 355-9400**
**Price:** **
**Atmosphere: Caribbean beach skyline**
**baragricole.com/**

This is the place to enjoy Caribbean-made rhum agricole with more than twenty mostly French Caribbean rums on the menu. This modern, very San Francisco–styled restaurant and bar serves some of the best drinks in the country and with the skyline of San Francisco as your backdrop, you'll head home grinning.

## La Folie

**2316 Polk St. San Francisco, CA 94109**
**(415) 775-5577**
**Price:** ***
**Atmosphere: Russian Hill French**
**lafolie.com/**

Depending on the time of day, order up a charcuterie plate, some salmon lollipops, or a basket of macarons to go with your Reverse Cosmosis made with St-Germain. White bar stools, cool mint walls, and a famous happy hour are the hallmarks of this popular French-feeling bar and resto.

# Florida

## Villa Azul

**309 23rd St., Miami Beach, FL 33139**
**(305) 763-8699**
**Price:** **
**Atmosphere: White hot**
**villaazurmiami.com/**

Saddle up to the bar and order a French Kiss, a Veev en Rose, or Mon Cheri at this white wonderland frequented by the who's who of Miami. So stylish, you'll want to move in and make a night of it.

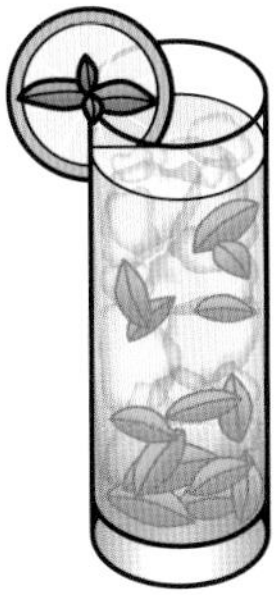

## Illinois

### Maude's Liquor Bar

**840 W. Randolph St., Chicago, IL 60607**
**(312) 243-9712**
**Price: ****
**Atmosphere: Brooklyn-style hipster**
**maudesliquorbar.com/**

A sparkling St-Germain fizz or a Lillet Rose will start you off at this dimly lit hipster enclave that feels more like Williamsburg, Brooklyn than Chicago. Downstairs serves more rustic fare while upstairs you'll find the finer more complex cocktails, either way you'll relish this seductive Chi-town hotspot.

## Massachusetts

### Les Zygomates

**129 South St., Boston, MA 02111**
**(617) 542-5108**
**Price: ****
**Atmosphere: Wine bar cool**
**winebar129.com/**

Yes, it's primarily a wine bar (Boston's finest) and a French bistro, but head to the bar and grab an Aviation with crème de Violette or their Champagne cocktail with house-made bitters and you'll understand the meaning of their name in French. Les Zygomates refers to the muscles in your face that allow you to smile.

"You can learn a lot about a woman by getting smashed with her."

*Tom Waits*

## Minnesota

### Coup D'Etat

**2923 Girard Ave. S., Minneapolis, MN 55408**
**(612) 354-3575**
**Price: ****
**Atmosphere: Minnesota party**
**coupdetatmpls.com/**

Emperor Napoleon hangs proudly in this huge, double-decker bar, restaurant, and party space in Minneapolis. Jesse, the head bartender, is considered the finest in the region, and the bar was named one of the best new openings in 2014, countrywide. The Ritz cocktail and grilled oysters with Pernod butter will make a homesick Francophile swoon.

## Pennsylvania

### The Good King Tavern

**614 S. 7th St., Philadelphia, PA 19147**
**(215) 625-3700**
**Price: ***
**Atmosphere: Casual pub**
**thegoodkingtavern.com/**

Old wooden bar, rustic French feel, tavern Fare, and classic French cocktails on offer. Settle into a French 75 or a Sazerac and let your hair down. Their motto: A whole lotta soul, some hip, some hop, and a really good time.

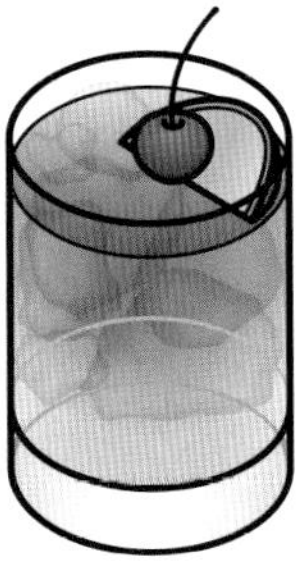

## Texas

### Julep

**1919 Washington Ave., Houston, TX 77707**
**(713) 869-4383**
**Price: ****
**Atmosphere: Southern French**
**julephouston.com/**

Considered one of the best bars to open in 2014, this gorgeously posh France-meets-the-south bar looks fresh and summery year round. They specialize in the oh-so-southern mint julep in every contortion. But owner and cocktail maven Alba Huerta also offers an Armagnac Sazerac, a Vieux Carré, and a Brandied French for those pining for Paris.

### Boulevardier

**408 N. Bishop Ave., Dallas, TX 75208**
**(214) 942-1828**
**Price: ****
**Atmosphere: A loft in Texas**
**dallasboulevardier.com/**

Head to this French-inspired bar and bistro that serves oysters alongside their Raised & Infused cocktail that highlights gin, thyme, Cointreau, and absinthe. The perfect way to start a night out on the town in Dallas's arts district.

## Washington

### Bastille Bar

**5307 Ballard Ave., Seattle, WA 98107**
**(206) 453-5014**
**Price: ****
**Atmosphere: Subway tile bistro**
**bastilleseattle.com/**

Head to the back bar, with its huge French chandelier and chocolate colored walls for a stylish night out in Seattle. Sample the Millionaire's punch with bourbon, absinthe, and grenadine, and slurp down some local oysters.

# — THE LAST WORD —

This cocktail comes to us from the maker of Chartreuse Verte but was invented in Detroit in 1920 at the Detroit Athletic club during Prohibition. It was forgotten about until Murray Stensen, a well-known bartender at the Zig Zag bar in Seattle, found it and brought it back into the current repertoire.

---

- **½ oz. Chartreuse Verte**
- **½ oz. Maraschino liqueur (Luxardo preferred)**
- **½ oz. gin**
- **½ oz. lime**

---

**METHOD:** Pour all ingredients into a cocktail shaker with ice.

**SERVING SUGGESTION:** Shake, strain, and serve in a cold coupe glass garnishing with a lime curl.

*La vie est belle.*

LIFE IS BEAUTIFUL.

## - Acknowledgments -

First I'd like to thank my editor, Alex Lewis of Cider Mill Press, who at a young age is the publishing director at an independent publishing firm in Maine. She picked me out of a sea of wonderful writers on the subject, thanks to the huge audience of Girls' Guide to Paris readers. So, in turn, I must thank our 1+ million readers who put our online Paris e-guide on the map. Alex was with me throughout giving creative suggestions and letting me immerse myself in the exciting new world of Parisian cocktails. I must also thank my intern and research assistant Ariana Mozafari who was critical to my being able to finish this book. It wouldn't have been nearly as fun without her by my side and at the bar.

Most of all I must thank my family: my husband, who is the finest male supporter of a female that has ever graced the earth, and my two twenty-something kids, who keep me current and support me in everything I do. Getting paid to drink and write about cocktails in Paris was truly a dream come true.

AGRICOLE
VARIOUS

2 Chevaux, 115
14 Julliet, 132
23 Jump Street, 103
100% Winter Vitamin, 51
400 Blows, The, 23
1789, 131
1802, 38

absinthe
Death in the Afternoon, 88
Joy Division, 261
Léa d'Asco, 116
Maison Absinthe Colada, 265
Moonflower, 217
Sazerac, 254
La Zézette, 69
Afterbulles, L,' 94
Alchimia Cocktail, 37
allspice liqueur
Red House Old Fashioned, 221
Amaro
Iggy, 215
ambiance, bars with superb, 52–53, 55
Amélie, 23
Amour à la Française, 20
Andy Wahloo, 184
anise liqueur
Sazerac, 254
apéritif, definition of, 12
Aperol
100% Winter Vitamin, 51
Apicius, L,' 53, 55
apple liqueur
Raphael, 59
Armagnac
2 Chevaux, 115
White Agave, 157
Audemus Century, 224
Avant Comptoir, L,' 93
Aviation, 100

B&B, 47
banana liqueur
La Sauvage Bee's Knees, 56
Bar 228 at the Meurice, 36
Bar Agricole, 271
Bar Bouchon, 268
Bar Hemingway at the Ritz Paris, 133
Bar Josephine at the Lutetia Hotel, 38
Baron of Brooklyn, 263
Baron Rouge, Le, 92
Bastille Bar, 274
Bastille Celebration, The, 86
Bastille Sour, The, 121
Belle Hortense, La, 52–53
Bénédictine
B&B, 47
De La Bretagne, 197
Singapore Sling, 113
Vieux Carré, 255
Bisous du Soleil, 70
bitters, definition of, 12
Black Point à la Française, 207
blackberry liqueur
Bramble & Queen, 119
Bloody Secret, 193
Bloody Umami, 245
Bluebird, 186
Bobo Parisien, 206
Bon, Olivier, 13–14
Bon Chic Bon Genre, Le (BCBG), 123
Bonal Quina
23 Jump Street, 103
1789, 131
Boulevardier, 274
Bouligny Tavern, 256
bourbon
Steve Casino, 204
see also whisky
Bramble & Queen, 119
brandy
Amour à la Française, 20
B&B, 47
Le Metro, 27
brandy, apple
Education Sentimentale, 172
Serendipiti, 87
Vin Chaud, 168
Le Woody Wood, 239
brandy, cherry
Singapore Sling, 113
Brenne Chai Toddy, 170
Burlesque, 231

cachaça
Baron of Brooklyn, 263
Romeo à Rio, 209
Le Woody Wood, 239
Café Moderne, 189
Calbar, Le, 208
Calvados
Education Sentimentale, 172
Serendipiti, 87
Vin Chaud, 168
Le Woody Wood, 239
Cambridge Public House, The, 228
Campari
Libertine, 222
The Smoky Spicy Margarita, 210
Candelaria, 189
cassis
Alchimia Cocktail, 37
Le Metro, 27
Castor Club, 192
Cerise Soir, 147
Chamber G&T, The, 104
Chambord
Burlesque, 231
Champagne
The Bastille Celebration, 86
Bisous du Soleil, 70
Bramble & Queen, 119
Champagne Stiletto, 28
Cranberry Sparkler, 169
Death in the Afternoon, 88
French 75, 30
French 75 Squared, 101
Kir St. Louis, 78
Mazarinette, 219

Old Cuban, 201
Paris Paris, 44
Raphael, 59
Serendipiti, 87
Sherry Cherie, 83
Treize-75, 31
Champagne bars, 94
Charles' Jasmine, 153
Charlie, Le, 159
Chartreuse/Chartreuse Verte
about, 8
Black Point à la Française, 207
Chartreuse Mule, 165
The Last Word, 275
Cherche-Midi, 267
cherry liqueur
Rose de Varsovie, 73
Chez Nous, 91
Choco Peat, 129
chocolate liqueur
Audemus Century, 224
Choco Peat, 129
Conquistador, La, 233
Ciel de Paris, 52
Cigarette After Sex, 181
Clown Bar, 91
Cocchi Americano
Audemus Century, 224
Cranberry Sparkler, 169
Sade's Taboo, 262
coffee liqueur
Choco Peat, 129
Highland Cream, 136
Coffee Old Fashioned, 236
Cognac
French 75, 30
Iggy, 215
Le Metro, 27
Ritz Sidecar, 33
Vieux Carré, 255
Vin Chaud, 168
Cointreau
Bisous du Soleil, 70
Joy Division, 261
L'Orange Passion, 150
Pomegranate Margarita, 173
Ritz Sidecar, 33
Rose de Varsovie, 73
Sade's Taboo, 262
Singapore Sling, 113
Combat, 192
Comptoir Generale, 232
Conquistador, La, 233
Conserverie, La, 6
Cookie Loves Shots, 34
CopperBay, 192
cordials, definition of, 12
Coup D'Etat, 273
Coupette, 240
Craddock, Harry, 6
craft bars, 177–178, 184, 186, 189, 192, 196, 198, 200, 202, 208, 211, 213–214, 216, 218, 220, 226–228
Cranberry Sparkler, 169
crème de banane
Baron of Brooklyn, 263
crème de cacao
Audemus Century, 224
Highland Cream, 136
crème de cassis
Amour à la Française, 20
crème de menthe
Maison Absinthe Colada, 265
crème de rose
Rosebud, 191
crème de violette
Aviation, 100
Night Bird, 223
Park Hyatt Purple Mojito, 43
Cros, Pierre-Charles, 13–14
curaçao
2 Chevaux, 115
Sherry Cherie, 83
Le Woody Wood, 239
Cynar
100% Winter Vitamin, 51

Danico, 196
de Gorianinoff, Romée, 6, 13–14
De La Bretagne, 197
Death in the Afternoon, 88
dijestif, definition of, 12
Dirty Dick, 196
dive bars, 158–159
Dokhans, Le, 94
Domaine de Canton
Le Bon Chic Bon Genre (BCBG), 123
Education Sentimentale, 172
Drambuie
Red House Old Fashioned, 221
Dubonnet Rouge
Moonflower, 217

eau de vie, pear
Vin Chaud, 168
Ebiniste du Vin, L,' 93
Éclair, L,' 55
Education Sentimentale, 172
elderflower cordial
Expérience 1, 199
elderflower liqueur
The Bastille Celebration, 86
The Bastille Sour, 121
French 75 Squared, 101
Kir St. Louis, 78
Paris Paris, 44
Pink Panther, 259
Esquisse No. 1, 230
Expérience 1, 199
Experimental Cocktail Club (ECC), 6, 13–14, 15, 198, 240, 267

Façon Maria, 238
Faluka, 194
Fifty Fifty, 200
Florida, 271
Folie, La, 271
Folie en Tête, La, 158
Forvm Cocktail, 120
Française, A La, 186
French 75 (bar), 256
French 75 (cocktail), 30
French 75 Squared, 101
French Manhattan, The, 122
French Martini de Nancy, 152
French Old Fashioned, The, 110
French Open Pimm's Cup, 134

French Paradox, The, 94
French White Negroni, 138
Fréquence, 200
Fuego de Colima, 229

galangal syrup
Alchimia Cocktail, 37
recipe, 37
Gaspar Brasserie, 270
Georges V, 35–36
gin
Audemus Century, 224
Aviation, 100
Bobo Parisien, 206
Bramble & Queen, 119
Burlesque, 231
The Chamber G&T, 104
Charles' Jasmine, 153
Cigarette After Sex, 181
Forvm Cocktail, 120
French 75 Squared, 101
French White Negroni, 138
Le Grand's Original Dry Martini, 135
Joy Division, 261
The Last Word, 275
Léa d'Asco, 116
Mazarinette, 219
Oh My Dog, 50
Picasso Martini, 140
Le Pulpeux, 234
Rosebud, 191
La Sauvage Bee's Knees, 56
Singapore Sling, 113
The Soirée, 146
Treize-75, 31
Verbena Cocktail, 40
Verdant Martini, 81
ginger beer
14 Julliet, 132
Chartreuse Mule, 165
ginger cordial
Old Cuban, 201
ginger liqueur
Amour à la Française, 20
Le Bon Chic Bon Genre (BCBG), 123
Education Sentimentale, 172
Glass, 202
Good King Tavern, The, 273
Gossima Ping Pong Bar, 232
Grand Hotel, Le, 133
Grand Marnier
Black Point à la Française, 207
Forvm Cocktail, 120
Grand's Original Dry Martini, Le, 135
grapefruit liqueur
French Martini de Nancy, 152
Kir St. Louis, 78
Rosé Pamp, 79
The Soirée, 146
Grenade liqueur
Oh My Dog, 50
grenadine, definition of, 13
Griottines juice
Cerise Soir, 147
Guêpe Verte, 190

Harry's Bloody Mary Recipe, The, 128
Harry's New York Bar, 127
hibiscus liqueur
The Last Call, 155
The Year of the Frenchman, 126
Highland Cream, 136
historic bars, 127, 133, 137
hotel bars, 35–36, 38, 42
Hôtel Particulier Bar, 71
hydromel
De La Bretagne, 197

Iced Tea Peyi, 64
Iggy, 215
Illinois, 272
ingredients, about, 10

Jean Lafitte's Old Absinthe House 1807, 257
Jefrey's, 202
Jennifer's Slipper, 154
Joy Division, 261
Julep, 274
Kahlua
Choco Peat, 129
see also coffee liqueur
King L'Avion d'Or
Bobo Parisien, 206
Kir St. Louis, 78

Lab, Le, 241
Lady B, 124
Lapérouse, 53
Last Call, The, 155
Last Word, The, 275
Léa d'Asco, 116
Libertine, 222
Lillet
23 Jump Street, 131
Lady B, 124
L'Orange Passion, 150
Lillet Blanc
Léa d'Asco, 116
Mistinguette, 106
liqueur, definition of, 12–13
Liqueur de Sapin Dolin
Piste Verte, 164
liqueur de violette
Romeo à Rio, 209
liquor, definition of, 13
Little Door, 268
Little Red Door, 214
London, 240
Los Angeles, 268–269
Lulu White, 216

Maison Absinthe Colada, 265
Maison Premiere, 264
maraschino liqueur
Aviation, 100
The Last Word, 275
Whisky Sour Cerise, 250
Maria Loca, 218
Martin, Stephen, 8
Martinique Shrubb liqueur
Cerise Soir, 147
Mary Celeste, Le, 211
Massachusetts, 272
Maude's Liquor Bar, 272
Mazarinette, 219
Meier, Frank, 6
Metro, Le, 27
mezcal

Cigarette After Sex, 181
The Smoky Spicy Margarita, 210
Midori
Jennifer's Slipper, 154
Minnesota, 273
Mistinguette, 106
Mon Oncle, 23
Monsieur Benjamin, 270
Montreal, 241
Moonflower, 217

Napoleon House, 257
New Orleans bars, 256–257
New York, 258, 264, 267
Night Bird, 223
Noix de la St Jean
Steve Casino, 204

Oh My Dog, 50
Old Cuban, 201
Orange Passion, L,' 150

Paris Paris, 44
Park Hyatt Purple Mojito, 43
Park Hyatt Vendome, 42
party menus, 66, 84–85, 109, 148–149, 166, 182–183, 252–253
pastis
about, 66
Seapea, 114
Peninsula Hotel, 36
Pennsylvania, 273
Perchoir, Le, 71
Pères Populaires, Les, 159
Picasso Martini, 140
Picon Club
Black Point à la Française, 207
Pimms' No. 1
French Open Pimm's Cup, 134
Pink Panther, 259
pisco
Faluka, 194
Piste Verte, 164
pomegranate liqueur
Pomegranate Margarita, 173
Pommeau de Bretagne
De La Bretagne, 197
port, tawny
Baron of Brooklyn, 263
Pour Vous, 269
Prescription Cocktail Club, 218
Prohibition, 6
Pulpeux, Le, 234

Quatre, Le, 48

Raphael, 59
Raphael Terrace, 58
raspberry cordial
Oh My Dog, 50
Recyclerie, La, 53
Red House, 220
Red House Old Fashioned, 221
Rehab, 220
rhum agricole
Cookie Loves Shots, 34
Iced Tea Peyi, 64
Maison Absinthe Colada, 265
Ritz Sidecar, 33
Romeo à Rio, 209
rose cordial
Oh My Dog, 50
Rose de Varsovie, 73
Rosé Pamp, 79
Rosebud, 137, 191
Royal Monceau, Le, 36, 38
rum
Façon Maria, 238
Fuego de Colima, 229
Iced Tea Peyi, 64
Old Cuban, 201
Park Hyatt Purple Mojito, 43
rye
Champagne Stiletto, 28
Red House Old Fashioned, 221
Sazerac, 254
Vieux Carré, 255
see also whisky
Sade's Taboo, 262
San Francisco, 269–271
Sauvage Bee's Knees, La, 56
Sazerac, 254
Sazerac Bar, The, 256
Scotch
Highland Cream, 136
Moonflower, 217
see also whisky
Seapea, 114
Serendipiti, 87
Shake N' Smash, 226
Shangri-La, 35
sherry, amontillado
Sherry Cherie, 83
Sherry Butt, 227
Simple Syrup, 10
Singapore Sling, 113
Sipsmith Summer Cup
Mazarinette, 219
Sister Midnight, 227
sloe gin/sloe gin liqueur
Mazarinette, 219
Smoky Spicy Margarita, The, 210
Société, La (LS), 241
Soirée, The, 146
Solera Paris, 228
Sorel
The Last Call, 155
The Year of the Frenchman, 126
Sour Mix, 154
Steve Casino, 204
St-Germain
The Bastille Celebration, 86
The Bastille Sour, 121
Bobo Parisien, 206
French 75 Squared, 101
Kir St. Louis, 78
Paris Paris, 44
Pink Panther, 259
substitutions, 10
Suze
Baron of Brooklyn, 263
French White Negroni, 138
Suze and Soda, 24
Syndicat, Le, 213

Tableau Bar & Bistro, 242
tequila
23 Jump Street, 103
Bloody Secret, 193
Coffee Old Fashioned, 236
Conquistador, La, 233
Fuego de Colima, 229
Guêpe Verte, 190
Jennifer's Slipper, 154
L'Orange Passion, 150
Pomegranate Margarita, 173
Texas, 274
thyme liqueur
Le Pulpeux, 234
Top of the Standard, The, 267
Toronto, 241
Tout-Paris, Le, 71
Treize-75, 31
Trieze au Jardin, 52
triple sec
Charles' Jasmine, 153
Joy Division, 261
L'Orange Passion, 150
Pomegranate Margarita, 173
Ritz Sidecar, 33
Singapore Sling, 113
Trou Normand, 269

umami
Bloody Umami, 245
Umami Martini, 243
unique bars, 232, 235
Urchin Bistrot, 270

Vancouver, 242
Velvet Falernum
Iced Tea Peyi, 64
Verbena Cocktail, 40
Verbena Cocktail, 40
Verdant Martini, 81
Verjus
Cigarette After Sex, 181
vermouth
23 Jump Street, 103
definition of, 13
Forvm Cocktail, 120
Picasso Martini, 140
Umami Martini, 243
vermouth, dry
French White Negroni, 138
Le Grand's Original Dry Martini, 135
Iggy, 215
Joy Division, 261
Verdant Martini, 81
vermouth, sweet
The French Manhattan, 122
Rosebud, 191
Sade's Taboo, 262
Vieux Carré, 255
Vieux Carré, 255
Villa Azul, 271
Vin Chaud, 168
vodka
100% Winter Vitamin, 51
Alchimia Cocktail, 37
Bisous du Soleil, 70
Choco Peat, 129
Esquisse No. 1, 230
Expérience 1, 199
French Martini de Nancy, 152
The Harry's Bloody Mary Recipe, 128
Libertine, 222
Mistinguette, 106
Paris Paris, 44
Picasso Martini, 140
Pink Panther, 259
Piste Verte, 164
Rose de Varsovie, 73
Zeitouni, 185

Wall St. Bar, 235
Washington, 274
whisky
14 Julliet, 132
1789, 131
The Bastille Celebration, 86
The Bastille Sour, 121
Black Point à la Française, 207
Le Bon Chic Bon Genre (BCBG), 123
Brenne Chai Toddy, 170
Choco Peat, 129
De La Bretagne, 197
The French Manhattan, 122
The French Old Fashioned, 110
Highland Cream, 136
Lady B, 124
The Last Call, 155
Léa d'Asco, 116
Night Bird, 223
The Smoky Spicy Margarita, 210
Whisky Sour Cerise, 250
The Year of the Frenchman, 126
see also bourbon; rye
White Agave, 157
wine, red
Vin Chaud, 168
wine, rosé
Rosé Pamp, 79
wine, white
1789, 131
Le Bon Chic Bon Genre (BCBG), 123
Esquisse No. 1, 230
La Zézette, 69
wine bars, 91–93
Woody Wood, Le, 239

Year of the Frenchman, The, 126

Zeitouni, 185
Zézette, La, 69
Zygomates, Les, 272

## - ABOUT THE AUTHOR -

*Doni Belau* first saw Paris at the tender age of eighteen and fell in love. She has been regularly visiting or living in her favorite city ever since. In 2009, Ms. Belau founded the website www.GirlsGuidetoParis.com, an insider's guide to the city of light. The site includes her hand-picked favorite restaurants, bars, hotels, apartments, and activities to experience Paris like a native. It also features blogs written by Ms. Belau and many other contributors, D.I.Y. walking tours, and the popular GO-Card for Paris-bound travelers. After six years, the site has grown to 1.5 million readers per year and is one of the foremost Anglophone guides for travelers to France. In 2014, Doni authored the online guidebook EAT in Paris. She divides her time between New York City, Paris, and the Bordeaux region, where she shares a home with her husband and two grown children.

## - ABOUT CIDER MILL PRESS BOOK PUBLISHERS -

Good ideas ripen with time. From seed to harvest, Cider Mill Press brings fine reading, information, and entertainment together between the covers of its creatively crafted books. Our Cider Mill bears fruit twice a year, publishing a new crop of titles each spring and fall.

CIDER MILL PRESS
BOOK PUBLISHERS

501 Nelson Place
Nashville, Tennessee 37214

cidermillpress.com

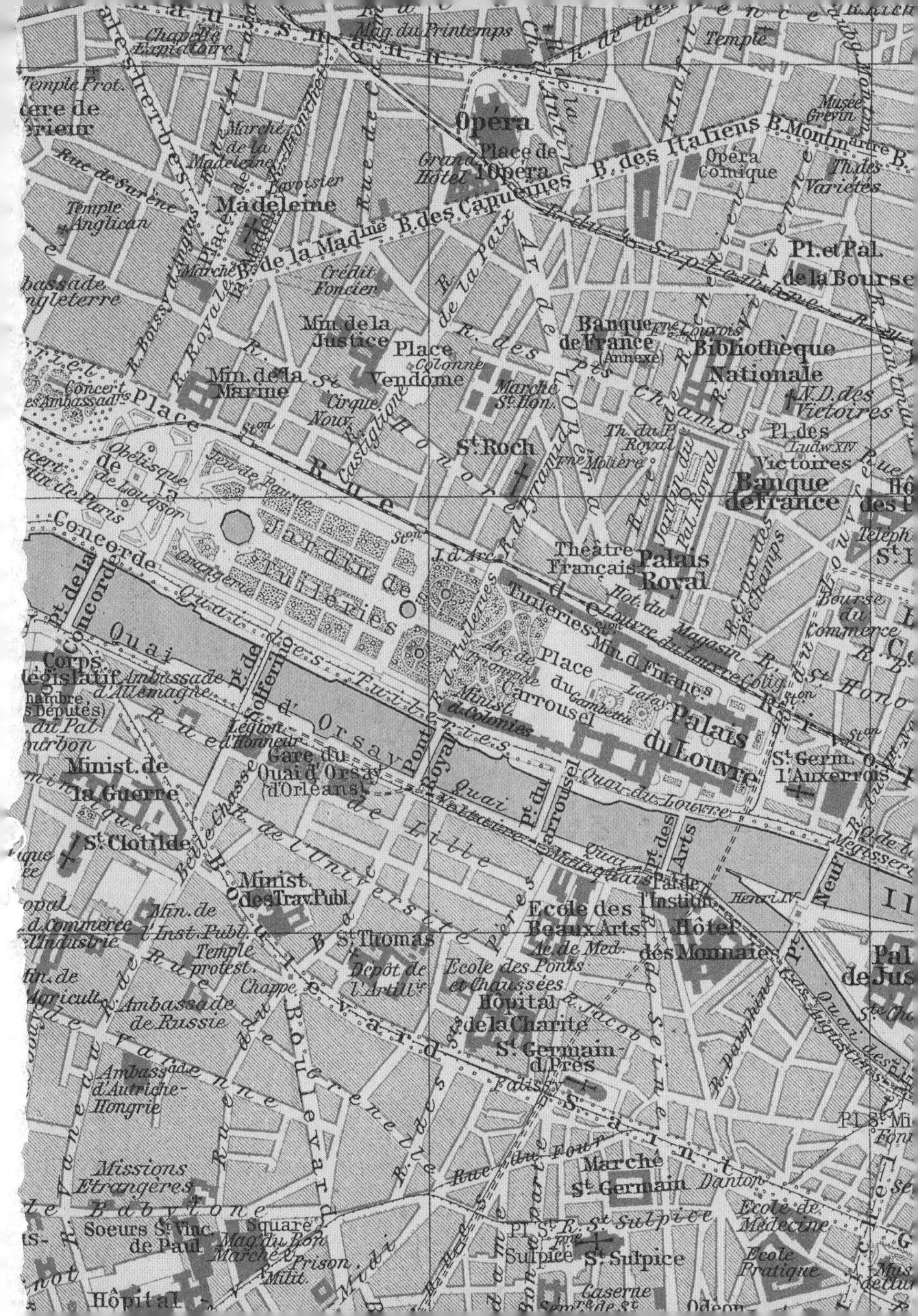

Chapelle Expiatoire
Mag. du Printemps
Temple
Temple Prot.
Opéra
Place de l'Opéra
Grand Hôtel
B. des Italiens
B. Montmartre
Opéra Comique
Th. des Variétés
Musée Grévin
Marché de la Madeleine
Madeleine
Temple Anglican
B. de la Mad.ne
B. des Capucines
R. du 4 Septembre
Pl. et Pal. de la Bourse
Crédit Foncier
Ambassade d'Angleterre
Min. de la Justice
Place Vendôme
Colonne
Banque de France (Annexe)
Bibliothèque Nationale
N. D. des Victoires
Min. de la Marine
Concert des Ambassad.rs
Cirque Nouv.
Marché St. Hon.
Th. du P. Royal
Pl. des Victoires
St. Roch
Banque de France
Obélisque
Jeu de Paume
Place de la Concorde
Jardin des Tuileries
Orangerie
Théâtre Français
Palais Royal
Jardin du Pal. Royal
Bourse du Commerce
Place du Carrousel
Arc de Triomphe du Carrousel
Min. d. Financ.
Palais du Louvre
St. Germ. l'Auxerrois
Pt. de la Concorde
Corps Législatif
Ambassade d'Allemagne
Pt. Solferino
Légion d'Honneur
Quai d'Orsay
Gare du Quai d'Orsay (d'Orléans)
Pont Royal
Quai des Tuileries
Quai du Louvre
Pt. du Carrousel
Pt. des Arts
Minist. de la Guerre
St. Clotilde
Quai Voltaire
Quai Malaquais
R. de l'Université
R. de Lille
Minist. des Trav. Publ.
Palais de l'Institut
Henri IV
Pt. Neuf
Min. de l'Inst. Publ.
St. Thomas
École des Beaux Arts
Hôtel des Monnaies
Temple protest.
Dépôt de l'Artill.
École des Ponts et Chaussées
Ac. de Méd.
Ambassade de Russie
Hôpital de la Charité
R. Jacob
St. Germain d. Prés
R. Dauphine
Quai des Augustins
Ambassade d'Autriche-Hongrie
Boulevard St. Germain
Missions Étrangères
Rue du Four
Marché St. Germain
Danton
R. de Babylone
Soeurs St. Vinc. de Paul
Square
R. St. Sulpice
École de Médecine
École Pratique
St. Sulpice
Prison Milit.
Hôpital
Caserne
Odéon

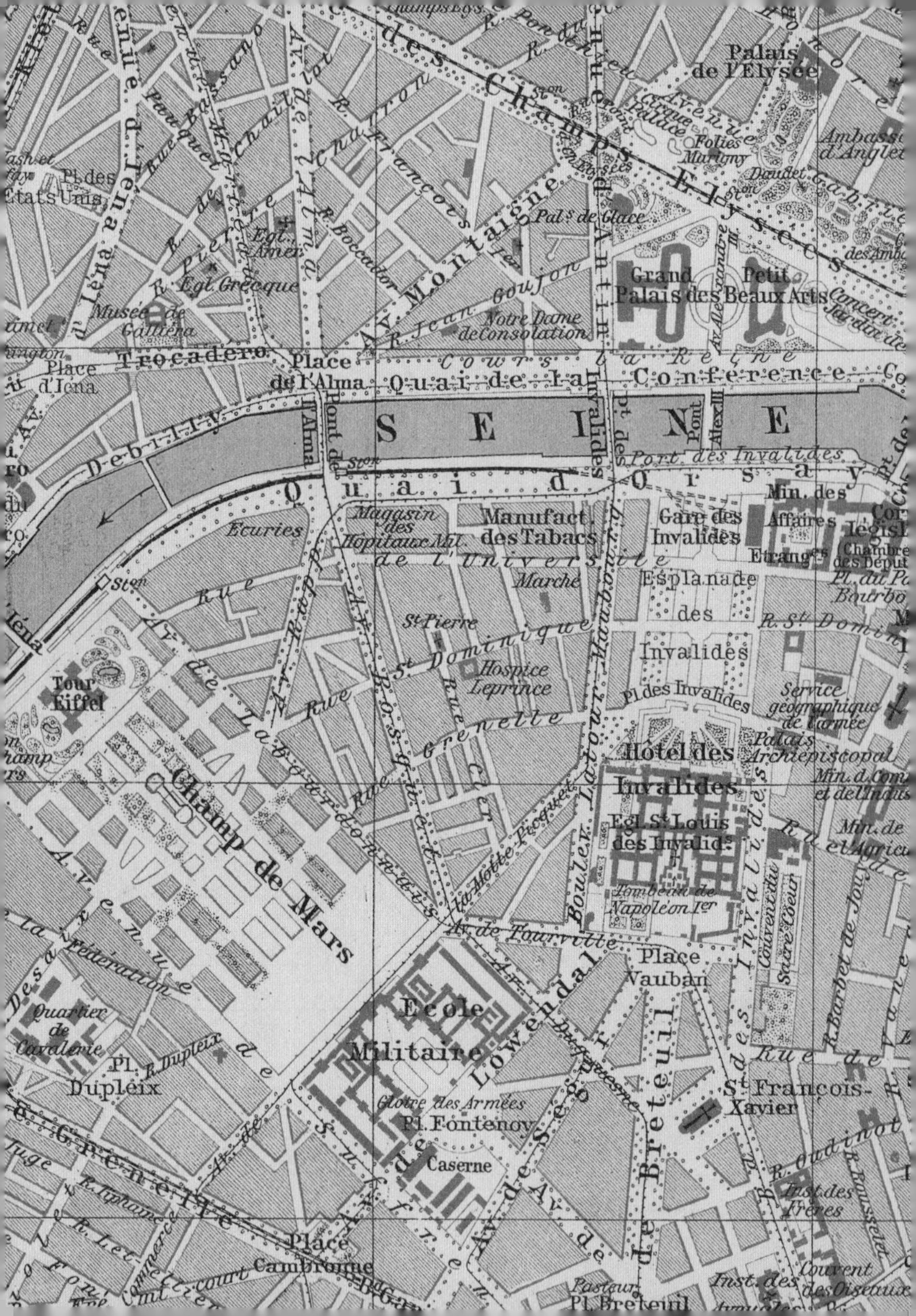
Palais de l'Elysée
Champs Elysées
Cirque Palace
Folies Marigny
Ambass. d'Anglet
Pl. des Etats Unis
Av. d'Iéna
R. de Chaillot
Egl. Amér.
Egl. Grecque
Musée de Galliéra
R. Boccador
Av. Montaigne
Pal. de Glace
R. Jean Goujon
Notre Dame de Consolation
Grand Palais des Beaux Arts
Petit
Av. Alexandre III
Trocadero
Place d'Iéna
Place de l'Alma
Cours la Reine
Quai de la Conférence
Pont de l'Alma
Pt. des Invalides
Pont Alex III
SEINE
Port des Invalides
Quai d'Orsay
Min. des Affaires Etrangères
Gare des Invalides
Manufact. des Tabacs
Magasin des Hôpitaux Mil.
Ecuries
Rue de l'Université
Marché
Esplanade des Invalides
R. St. Dominique
St Pierre
Hospice Leprince
Rue St Dominique
Rue de Grenelle
Pl. des Invalides
Service géographique de l'armée
Palais Archiépiscopal
Tour Eiffel
Av. de La Bourdonnais
Av. Rapp
Av. Bosquet
Rue Cler
Champ de Mars
Hôtel des Invalides
Egl. St. Louis des Invalid.
Tombeau de Napoléon Ier
Boulev. Latour Maubourg
Av. de La Motte Picquet
Av. de Tourville
Place Vauban
Boulev. des Invalides
Couvent du Sacré Coeur
R. Barbet de Jouy
Min. de l'Agricult.
Ecole Militaire
Av. de Lowendal
Av. de Ségur
Av. de Breteuil
Av. de la Fédération
Av. de Suffren
Quartier de Cavalerie
Pl. Dupleix
R. Dupleix
Gloire des Armées
Pl. Fontenoy
Caserne
St. François-Xavier
R. Oudinot
R. Rousselet
Inst. des Frères
Boulev. de Grenelle
Place Cambronne
R. du Commerce
Pl. Breteuil
Couvent des Oiseaux